GUITAR WORLD PR...

MW01130966

Dimebag Darrell's RIFFER MADNESS

by DIMEBAG DARRELL
with Nick Bowcott

An in-depth dissection of
Dimebag Darrell's
groundbreaking guitar style

"Crank your rig on 12, let it feedback wide-open for a good two minutes, freak your neighbors out and ENJOY THE POWER OF THE GUITAR! 'Oh, what a feeling,' and it ain't no damned Toyota!"

Dimebag Darrell

Special thanks to Kim Zide of Concrete Management for her assistance with this project.

The accompanying CD was recorded by Nick Bowcott on a Korg D1600 digital recorder, using ESP, Jackson and Fender guitars and Seymour Duncan JB pickups. The guitars were plugged into either a Marshall JMP-1 (the ultimate preamp), Korg AX1500G or a Line 6 POD.

WARNER BROS. PUBLICATIONS
Warner Music Group
An AOL Time Warner Company
USA: 15800 NW 48th Avenue, Miami, FL 33014

IMP
INTERNATIONAL MUSIC PUBLICATIONS LIMITED
ENGLAND: GRIFFIN HOUSE,
161 HAMMERSMITH ROAD, LONDON W6 8BS

Edited and Compiled by Nick Bowcott
Special thanks to Brad Tolinski and everyone at Guitar World
Project Manager: Aaron Stang
Cover Design: Nancy Rehm
Cover Photo: Joe Giron
Interior Design and Layout: Dianne S. Walker
Engraver: Musical/Arts Consultants, Inc.
Technical Editor: Jack Allen
Text Editor: Nadine DeMarco

Foreword

The Birth of a Metal God

Thankfully, every now and then the rock world is blessed with the birth of a new guitarist who not only thrills us with ungodly playing but inspires others to wanna play better too. Such rare individuals are quickly anointed Guitar Gods by their adoring fans. To truly achieve Guitar God status though, groundbreaking chops alone are not enough—being able to consistently write world-class material is also an essential pre-requisite. Eric Clapton, Jeff Beck, Jimi Hendrix (RIP), Ritchie Blackmore, Jimmy Page, Tony Iommi, Randy Rhoads (RIP) and Edward Van Halen are all deserving of their "Guitar God" standings for the reasons just mentioned.

In the minds of many, mine included, a Texan wildman with a purple goatee and a penchant for making harmonics squeal like a pig, is the most exciting rock guitarist to have surfaced since Edward Van Halen. His name? Dimebag Darrell. His band? Pantera. When you listen to Dime's fiery fretwork on tracks like "Cemetary Gates" (Cowboys From Hell), "Shedding Skin" (Far Beyond Driven) or "Revolution Is My Name (Reinventing The Steel), it's easy to understand why. In addition to being one of the heaviest riff-mongers to ever prowl this planet, Darrell's lead work displays all the essential ingredients of a true metal master— melody, emotion, invention and a truly vulgar display of power!

In addition to being able to walk the walk, as you'll quickly discover in the pages that follow, Dime can also talk the talk. His streetwise, no-nonsense words of wisdom have motivated a multitude of guitarists the world over, myself included—hence the countless hours I've happily poured into this project. I sincerely hope that this book does Dime the justice he deserves because he truly has reinvented the steel and taken it to a new level! In so doing, Dime has deservedly earned induction into the hallowed ranks of bona fide Guitar Gods.

"Remember, it's all good, everything goes and there ain't no damned rules or boundaries. So get off! Tear it a fresh ass, tear it hard, rip gaping holes in it! Make tracks, leave marks!

"Forever stronger than all."

Dimebag Darrell

Introduction
"What the *#$%?"
Why & how this book was written

PART I: *Why are you doing this?*

Why dedicate an entire book to Dimebag Darrell? If, after reading my foreword, you're still dumb/deaf (delete as you deem fit!) enough to dare ask such an asinine question, please shut up, sit down and read on. As you'll quickly discover, the only question this book will raise is "Why the hell wasn't it written years ago?"

No More Heroes

When the history of heavy metal is written, the 1990s will be known as "*the decade of great riffs but no new lead guitar heroes—except one: Dimebag Darrell of Pantera.*" Wow, that's a bold statement to make, isn't it? But guess what, amigo? It's the truth, goddamn it, and a sad truth at that. Don't believe me? Well, take a deep breath, cast your mind back to that bygone era and then think long and hard about what I've just said. I'll bet you a beer or five that you'll come to the exact same conclusion I did: Loads of memorable new metal riffs but no *new* lead guitar rippers—aside from Dime, of course.

IMPORTANT NOTE: Just in case the above has got you all pissed-off at me and screaming, "But what about Kirk Hammett, Zakk Wylde, Marty Friedman, Eddie Van Halen, Kerry King and Jeff Hanneman, you moron? They're all ripping lead guitarists who blazed throughout the '90s!" Well, please allow me to clarify—all those "Metal Gods" rose to prominence in the '80s, not the '90s. So, even though they all continued to spew splendid solos in the '90s, they don't qualify as "*new guys!*" Geddit?

As we all know, despite the fact that certain self-proclaimed experts proclaimed that "metal was dead," killer metal riffs were in abundance pretty much throughout the '90s. "Veteran" acts such as Metallica, Megadeth, Slayer, Judas Priest and even a reunited "original" Black Sabbath (one of the definite highlights of the decade!) continued to pedal their praiseworthy wares. And "newcomers" like Alice in Chains, Korn, Fear Factory, Stone Temple Pilots, White Zombie, Prong, the Deftones and Rage Against the Machine (to name but a few) also delivered the metal goods in fine fashion too. The trouble was, hardly any of the new guys were playing lead. In fact, if anything, most of 'em were totally "anti-lead" and avoided soloing like the plague. Hell, some of them even went public with their "solos suck" stance!

Thankfully Dimebag was having none of this, and even though every Pantera song doesn't contain an obligatory lead break, his soloing on each of the six albums the band put out in the '90s was both breathtaking and welcome!

Public Opinion: *Dime Rules!*

The distinct lack of new lead guitar gods in the '90s was reflected in the "Best Heavy Metal Guitarist" polls in guitar magazines the world over. Two guys ruled supreme—Metallica's Kirk Hammett, who's been dominating said polls since the mid '80s, and the only "new guy" seemingly not afraid to blaze, Dimebag. Pantera's major label debut, "Cowboys From Hell," came out in 1990 and by 1992 Dime had become a front-runner in the "Best Heavy Metal" stakes in the guitar magazines' annual reader's polls. Ten years and six albums later, Dime remains the people's champion, not only winning the "Best Hard Rock/Heavy Metal Guitarist" reader's poll awards with alarming consistency but also getting a few "Most Valuable Player" awards under his belt too.

My Humble Opinion: *Dime Rules*

Read my foreword—again!

Defenders of the Faith

Along with soloing, another big '90s taboo was any association with the term *heavy metal*. Self-appointed music press "experts" declared the genre dead and countless bands denied it in a fashion of which Judas would've been proud. "We're not ****in' heavy metal," the guilty ones declared in droves, despite the fact that their dissonant 'n' doomy, tuned-down riffage had "we were weaned on Black Sabbath" written all over it!

Thankfully, once again, Dimebag Darrell and Pantera were having none of that nonsense and quite literally screamed their undying allegiance to metal from sold-out stadium stages all over the world. "We've always said that we're proud to be a metal band and we always will," Dime affirms. "I grew up a heavy metal kid, listening to great metal bands, and that's what we've always dreamed of being. Metal isn't a haircut, it's an attitude, and I know it's not real fashionable right now but we ain't about to let anyone down—we ain't about to deny what we are just so we can sell more records. We play extreme music and we love the heavy shit so why would we do anything else than what we're best at?! It kills me when I see other metal bands trying to pass themselves off as something else just because metal isn't in style at the moment. Well, brother, they can join the pack, 'cos we're gonna remain true to our roots while all that other shit keeps twisting around us. We're like a steel rod and we won't bend. We're just gonna get bigger, stronger and harder. We're the full-meal deal, man—we're all about kick-ass songs with lead vocals, lead guitar, over-the-top drumming, killer bass lines and a shitload of no-holds-barred heavy riffs you can bust a nut on!

"It doesn't matter what the 'experts' say, this form of music will *never* go away," our subject continues, his eyes ablaze with passion and sincerity. "Trends can come and go 'cos we're gonna keep playing right through them. To me, a trend is kinda like a zit, except people think trends are cool—they both grow and grow and then finally, POP! They burst and go back to their normal size. So, it don't matter how many zits spring up around us 'cos we know they ain't gonna be around forever and we'll still be there when they're gone. This band is like a mole—a bad-assed, nasty mole—and we ain't even halfway to where we're going!"

Judging by the vast legions of fans that flock to Pantera concerts and the impressive array of platinum and gold disks that adorn the walls of Dimebag's pad, Camp Strapped, the band's unbending metal stance has clearly paid off. What is more, Pantera is clearly nowhere near being done. "We're just starting to get real good at what we do!" Dime laughs. "We're four guys who are like family—we're in love with what we do and we're on fire when we're touring, man. We ain't never gonna stop; we're the Rolling Stones of the heavy shit! And we'll never, ever change; there's no reason to—I can't see how it could ever change and that's the god's honest truth."

Amen! Long live the "bad-assed, nasty mole."

Credit Where Credit Is Due

Not surprisingly, the world's guitar press was quick to notice the impact Dime was having on young players, and he's deservedly adorned countless covers as a result. Of all the praise that has been heaped on our subject by such publications, the most succinct of all appeared in the February 1997 issue of *Guitar World* in which the following passage appeared:

Pantera's "King Dime" is the premier metal guitarist of the Nineties. In an age when most headbangers have packed up their gig bags and moved to greener, grungier pastures, Darrell continues to dish out some of the decade's most brutal and uncompromising thrash. By combining the virtuosity of Edward Van Halen with the hyperactive rhythmic drive of a glue-sniffin' punk guitarist, Darrell has created a style that appeals to classic rockers, fans of death metal and industrial afficionados as well.

Part II: *How?*

In 1993, *Guitar World*, the biggest-selling guitar magazine on the planet, decided to see if they could get three of the hottest lead players on the planet to pen some columns for 'em. Their first two choices were no-brainers—Kirk Hammett and Eric Johnson, both firmly established as giants amongst the six-string elite. Finding the third guy, however, was gonna be a little less obvious. *Guitar World's* editor, Brad Tolinski, didn't want to take the easy route and give it to someone who was already firmly established as a household name, y'see. Instead he wanted to take a risk and give it to a relative unknown—a player whose star was on the rise but wasn't clearly visible for all to see yet. In short, it was a crapshoot.

Brad called me and asked me if I had any thoughts on the matter. In my mind there was no doubt who should get the gig, and so my answer was instant: "Dime's your man," I blurted. "I'd bet my house on it—if only I had one!" Brad and his crack editorial staff conferred and agreed. Furthermore, they offered me the task of being the writer who worked with Dime on his column—should he decide to accept this daunting mission. Thankfully he did and in the April 1993 issue of *Guitar World*, Dime's column made its auspicious debut. Its title? Fittingly enough, it was...

Riffer Madness

Like pretty much everything he does, be it writing, performing, playing or drinking(!), Dime took his *Guitar World* column incredibly seriously and labored over each and every word it contained. This was no ghostwritten affair with an anonymous writer literally putting words in the mouth of the supposed "author." Instead, Dime dotted every damned "i" and crossed every darned "t" in each and every column—which is exactly as it should be when any artist puts his or her name on a written piece. What a concept! I'd say that Dime dedicated at least four hours to each 750-word column. Here's the skinny on what would typically happen:

Darrell would pick a topic several months in advance and then we'd discuss it three or four times over the next two months to ensure I got tape of him looking at the same thing from slightly different angles. That done, I'd transcribe all his thoughts, rough out a column and send it to him. He'd then dick with it for a week or so and then we'd spend a good two hours on the phone making sure that every single word was perfect—regardless of where he was in the world. Can you say "far beyond dedicated"? Hell yeah, brother!

In short, if you liken *Riffer Madness* to recording an album, then Dime wrote, arranged, produced and mixed the whole darned thing. All I did was engineer the sucker—namely hit "record" when required and made sure nothing got lost or overlooked. At the risk of sounding like a kiss-ass, I don't mind telling you that it was a pleasure working with Dime on *Riffer Madness*—not only was it a lotta fun, I learned a bunch of cool stuff and I even got paid for my "troubles"! Sometimes life is good.

Dimebonics

As a direct result of Dime's dedication, *Riffer Madness* became incredibly popular with *Guitar World's* readers the world over. In addition to being crammed full of great playing ideas and advice, his column was unique in terms of both its no-bullshit, street-savvy approach and Dime's distinctive turn-of-phrase. Dime-isms like "crack a nut and undulate," "stay driven, keep your amps overdriven and flat-ass, straight-out jam," "bust your sack" and "don't go out there and just pitter about—stomp some ass motherf***er" would crack smiles in tens of thousands of homes each and every month. In fact, Darrell's colorful use of the English language inspired a good pal of mine, Jon Chappell, to come up with the term *Dimebonics*. Jon used this amusing term as the title of his "Opening Act" editorial when Dime adorned the cover of the May 1999 issue of *Guitar* magazine—a publication of which he was editor-in-chief at the time.

Letters praising *Riffer Madness* and requesting topics to be covered poured into *Guitar World's* NYC headquarters quite literally by the sackful. Furthermore, the vast majority of 'em contained Dime-isms culled from the column. Hell, one guy even sent in a picture of his dog sporting a purple goatee! The name of his mutt? Dimebag of course! Such was the devotion of countless *Riffer Madness* fans.

In total, Dime penned a staggering 28 columns for *Guitar World*, and when his final column appeared in the September '95 issue, flags were flown at half-mast and black armbands were donned by his vast throng of loyal readers. In addition to being a highly entertaining read y'see—as Dime so aptly put it in his fond, handwritten farewell—*Riffer Madness* offered up a "buttload of cool techniques, knowledge and straight-out crazy shit!!! Including some trick stuff I'm sure most blacksmiths would never reveal or uncover."

In addition to having the immense good fortune of working alongside Dime on his 28 *Riffer Madness* columns, I've also interviewed him more times than I care to remember and have conducted several "Private Lessons" with him for *Guitar World* too. As a result, I have a retardedly large library of Dime's wisdom and riffage on paper, tape and video. It is from this vast collection of knowledge (which I keep under lock and key!) that this book was born.

I'm sure you'll be delighted to learn that wherever and whenever possible, I let Dime do all the talking. Thanks to the superb job he did in his 28 columns, this was rarely a problem! I sincerely hope that reading *Riffer Madness* gives you as much pleasure as putting it all together gave me.

Table of Contents

PAGE   CD TRACK

FOREWORD: Reinventing the Steel 2
The birth of a metal god

INTRODUCTION: "What the *%#@?" 3
Why and how this book was written

CHAPTER 1: Plan of Attack 8
Dime's baseball analogy
        Example 1: "Mouth for War" intro riff 1

CHAPTER 2: We'll Grind That Axe for a Long Time...11
A brief summary of the Pantera story so far

CHAPTER 3: What Makes Dime Pick 19
A quick look at some of Dime's most prominent influences

CHAPTER 4: The Tone Zone 24
Dime's axes, amps 'n' FX

CHAPTER 5: Warming Up...31
        Examples 2–5 3–6

CHAPTER 6: First Base: Riffs...34
A detailed look at Dime's unique form of rhythm 'n' bruise
        Example 6: Palm Muting 7
        Example 7: The Ups and Downs of Picking. 8
        Example 8: Going Down 9
        Examples 9–11: Percussive Picking 10–12
        Examples 12–17: Psychotic Syncopation & Power Grooves. 13–15
        Examples 18–22: Holes of Silence (two-handed muting). 16–19
        Examples 23–28: Chromatic Man 20–24
        Examples 29–40: Bends 25–33
        Examples 41–46: Sinister Slides 34–39
        Example 47: Inverted Power Chords 40
        Examples 48–50: Skitzed-out Power Chords & the Tritone Interval 41–42
        Examples 51–53: Major and Minor Diads. 43–44
        Examples 54–57: Evil Intervals. 45–48
        Examples 58–60: Mr. Clean. 49–51
        Examples 61–63: Pedal to the Metal 52–54
        Examples 64–65: Odd Time Signatures 55–56
        Examples 66–69: Octave Repeats 57–60
        Examples 70–74: Going for Girth 61–62
        Examples 75–79: "Feedback Sack" Answers 63–66

CHAPTER 7: First-Base Revision..75
A detailed look at the rhythm work in "5 Minutes Alone"

    Examples 80–87 67–74

CHAPTER 8: Second Base: Leads 81
An in-depth look at some of Dime's lead-playing traits

    Examples 88–89: Stretches From Hell. 75
    Examples 90–92: Awkwardly Cool Runs 76–78
    Examples 93–99: Q&A 79–84

CHAPTER 9: Second-Base Revision 91
A detailed dissection of three killer Dime leads

    Example 100: "5 Minutes Alone" Solo 85
    Examples 101–102: "I'm Broken" Solo 86–87
    Example 103: "Floods" Outro Solo 88

CHAPTER 10: Third Base: The "Noise Factor"..101
"Harmonics and a whammy bar? These two things definitely go hand in hand if you ask me!"

    Examples 104–113: Harmonics, Whammy Bars, Echos and More 89–98

CHAPTER 11: Rut-Busting...111
Advice from Dime on how to dig out of a playing rut successfully

    Example 114 99

CHAPTER 12: Dear Dime..113
Dime answers a few FAQs (frequently asked questions) from his infamous Feedback Sack!

EPILOGUE: Uplift and C-Cut!...116
Unlucky for us, the end of the book! A parting inspirational shot from Dime as he say, "Lata!"

APPENDIX I: Discography 117

APPENDIX II: About the author plus the usual special thanks and acknowledgments...122

Chapter I

Plan of Attack

Dime's baseball analogy

As just mentioned, this book is gonna be based on the huge heap of Dime material I've amassed over the last ten years. (Damn, time flies when you're having fun, doesn't it?) It's a daunting pile o' stuff though and, as Darrell would say, "It's all good." So, the 64,000-dollar question is: How the hell do I arrange it all? Thankfully, in a fairly recent interview with Dime I asked him what he "considered a well-rounded player to be," and his answer was so freakin' good I immediately decided that it was gonna form the foundation upon which this book is written! Here's what he said:

My definition of a well-rounded player? Well, dude, I could put it a million different ways and here's just one of 'em. I like to cover all bases, and first base would definitely have to be riffs—in my book, if you don't have a riff, you don't have a song! Second base for guitar players is probably playing solos. Third base is the noise factor. Then, when you hit home, you've got all three of 'em and you put a little more into it too—a little feedback and a little bit of whatever else comes out too....let it all through, man, it's all good!

And there you have it, dear reader, from the lips of the man himself! So, the three main playing sections of this book are as follows:

First Base: Riffs
Second Base: Solos
Third Base: The Noise Factor

In addition to the above, as the Table of Contents page has already revealed, we're also gonna take a close-up look at Dimebag's rig, discuss his influences and also take a quick peek at the Pantera story thus far, including a detailed discography **(Appendix 1)**.

To whet your appetite for some of the playing techniques we're gonna be covering, check out **Example 1,** which is the opening salvo of "Mouth for War" *(Vulgar Display of Power)*. You can hear this on **Track 1** of the accompanying CD. This 24-bar excerpt features chromatic movement, syncopation, palm-muting, pedaling the root, short and "long-assed" chord slides and a cool use of natural harmonics to create what Dime describes as "a high-pitched percussive sound that gives the riff an extra dimension." We're gonna be checking out all of these techniques plus a whole lot more (like the harmonic squeal I've added to the end of CD **Track 1**) in the pages that follow.

Example 1: "Mouth for War" intro.

Guitar tuned to concert pitch (A = 440 Hz) (low to high: E A D G B E)

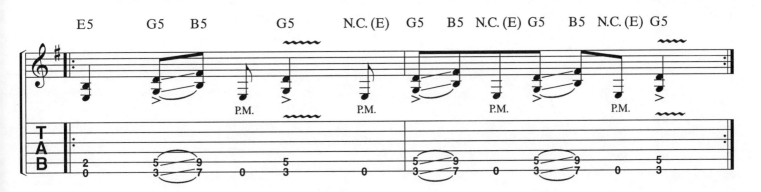

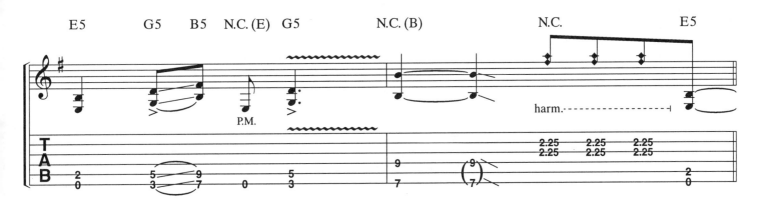

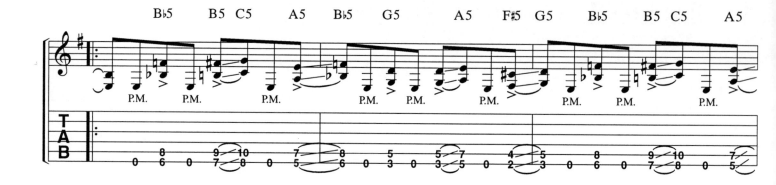

Goddamn, we've got a lot of ground to cover so, without any further ado, let's get right to it. As Dime stated at the very start of his first ever *Riffer Madness* column: "We're gonna be talking about practicing and jammin' with other people; hard-driving power grooves; percussive picking; getting out of ruts; harmonics and makin' them squeal; soloing ideas; bending chords; and some other stuff too. So let's plug in and start wailin'!"

Chapter 2

We'll Grind That Axe for a Long Time

A brief summary of the story of Dime 'n' Pantera so far . . .

Over the last ten years or so, Dime has done dozens of in-depth interviews for guitar magazines, many of them cover stories. As a result, both his story and Pantera's have been well beyond documented. So, in spite of the fact that this chapter could easily fill this entire book (and then some!), I'm gonna keep this historical look-back brief—well, the *Cowboys From Hell* to *Reinventing the Steel* era anyway!

The Cradle Will Rock

Dime was born Darrell Lance Abbott on Saturday, August 20, 1966, in Dallas, Texas, USA. His father, Jerry, was a professional musician who played in many bands, many clubs, and on many records but was mainly a studio engineer and ran a pretty successful recording operation in Pantego, Texas, called Pantego Sound Studios. Although some fathers have a natural tendency to pressure their sons into following in their footsteps, Jerry (a.k.a. The Eld'n) did no such thing—instead he let nature take its course. According to Dime, "I wouldn't say he encouraged me, but the opportunity for me to be a musician was always there. I think my Dad might have been a little reluctant to push me into music because he'd seen enough of the rock 'n' roll lifestyle to know it's probably not the best thing to pursue! I guess it would be a bit like him saying, 'Here, son, go sell your soul to the devil.' That's not necessarily something you'd want for your kid! Y'know that phrase, 'sold your soul for rock 'n' roll'? It ain't bullshit, man!"

The fact that his father would let young Dime watch him at work in his studio definitely fueled a fire in his son's furtive mind though. "I really dug going down there and seeing great Texan blues guitarists like Bugs Henderson and Jimmy Wallace gettin' it on," our subject admits. "When I was about nine or ten years old I used to go down there as much as I could; it was awesome." This all said, around that time Dime was given the chance to get his first axe, and he turned down.

"On my tenth or eleventh birthday my Dad said to me, 'Son, you can either have a BMX bike or you can have this,' and he pointed to a guitar," Darrell recalls with a wry smile. "I ended up taking the goddamned bike, but a seed was definitely planted! Then I discovered Ace Frehley and Black Sabbath and it was all over, man! I went back to my old man and told him, so he got me a Les Paul copy and a Pignose amp for my next birthday.

"Initially I wasn't really playing the thing though; instead I was just using my guitar as a prop," Darrell continues. "Y'know, I'd skip school, put on my Kiss makeup and play air guitar in the mirror while *Alive!* was cranking! But then, when I was jacking around on it one day, I sussed out how to play the 'Smoke on the Water' riff [*Machinehead*, Deep Purple] using just single notes on the low E string, and that definitely got me all fired up about playing! Then my Dad showed me how to play a moveable power chord shape, and that made the riff sound heavy as shit. That whole song is living, ass-stompin' proof that you can take just three or four notes and come up with something that's totally bad-assed! Being able to play a whole song is one of the most satisfying things when you're learning to play guitar. Everybody can hum a tune, but to be able to sit down and play one was exciting as all hell—it still is."

After mastering this classic Deep Purple song, Dime set about learning the main riffs from "Cocaine" by Eric Clapton and Boston's "More Than a Feeling." The real turning point in his fledgling career as a guitarist, however, was a stomp box. "I got hold of an Electro-Harmonix Big Muff fuzz pedal," Darrell remembers with a wicked gleam in his eye. "Man, as soon as I discovered distortion and feedback it was all over—that was definitely *all she wrote!*"

Seeing that his son was serious about the guitar, Dime's dad was quick to pitch in with a few more pointers. "He's a really well-rounded musician and he taught me a lot," Darrell states. "He showed me a few different chord inversions and a major scale, a minor scale and the pentatonic blues scale too. I also learned how to pick things off records from him. I used to bring him albums and he'd pick out riffs and show them to me." Aside from such informal lessons from his father, Dime is 100% self-taught. "I did take one lesson when I was in a rut though," he confesses. "This dude showed me a weird-assed scale, wrote it out and then told me to practice it for a whole week before coming back for another lesson and showing him how well I'd nailed it. I took it home, but after a few minutes of that I went, "**** this, I wanna jam," and I never went back for that second lesson. I just don't have the patience for that kinda regimented shit. Hell, I don't even have the patience to read the newspaper—I'll read three or four lines and then I'm done, dude. I'm a spazzer, y'know?"

By Demons Be Driven

"Spazzer" or not, by the time Darrell was 13 years old, honing his six-string skills had become an all-consuming passion. "I was totally driven; the guitar was all I really gave a damn about, " Dime confirms. "For the next four or five years I skipped a shitload of school and just sat in my room and busted ass on my chops. That's all I did, man." In addition to jamming for hours on end, Dime would also learn by watching and talking to the guitarists who frequented his dad's studio and the local music store. "Sometimes I'd ask 'em to show me the hot lick of the day or I'd just pay real close attention to what they were doing," he reveals. "Then I'd take it home, dick with it to see how many ways I could stretch it. Doing that would always lead me into some new shit. That's how I learned, by twisting stuff around and trying to turn it into my own thing. Sometimes I learn new things by trying to play something, making a mistake and finding the beauty in it!

"I'm not heavy on theory or reading music books," he continues. "And, like I've just told you, I only know two or three scales. There are some guys out there who know every scale known to man, but if they ain't playing from the gut like they mean every note, then it might just as well be a computer spewing out the notes. I'll take one note played with feel, guts and heart over a million others any day, man. The Reverend G, Billy Gibbons, is the true master of that shit."

Winner Takes All

The young axeman's dedication to his chosen craft clearly paid off because he started entering regional Hottest Guitar Player in Texas types of contests and won every darned one he took part in! As a result, Dime won several guitars including a Dean ML—the shape of which he is now synonymous with. He also won another piece of gear from one of his competition triumphs that would play an important role in the creation of his now instantly recognizable signature sound—a Randall solid-state RG100 half stack.

"Everything just seemed to start to happen because of fate or maybe just good karma," Dime recollects with a satisfied grin. "I had just won my first Dean and then I won the RG100 half stack. As soon as I plugged in I knew it was the amp for me; it sounded like a goddamned chainsaw! I heard something different in it right off the bat, and I figured that given some time I could make my own tone out of it.* It really had some balls but it wasn't quite perfect, it was a little fuzzy-sounding. So, I tried cleaning the sound up a little bit with one of those blue MXR six-band equalizers. Man, it was like night and day! That little blue stomp box is the shit! I've tried the other equalizers MXR makes, but none of 'em affect my sound in the same way. I've got to have the blue one."

*Note: For more information concerning Dime's gear, both past and present, see **Chapter 3.**

Unfortunately for Dime, but fortunately for the other young Texan guitarists around at the time, after seven straight Best Rock Guitarist competition wins, the organizers forced him into early retirement. "They said to me, 'Look, man, you've already won a bunch. Let someone else get a shot!'" Darrell laughs.

He's Heavy, He's My Brother

Another factor that definitely played a significant role in Dime's formative years as a guitarist was the fact that his older brother and fellow founding member of Pantera, Vinnie Paul, plays the drums. "One day Vinnie came back from school with a ****in' tuba!" Darrell laughs. "My old man said, 'Son, you won't be able to make a penny playing that thing. Take it back and tell 'em that you're gonna play the drums!'" Vinnie did exactly that and, as the saying goes, the rest of the story is now a part of modern hard rock history.

As it happens, the Abbott brothers aren't the only pair of guitar-and-drum-playing siblings in a world-famous rock band—a certain Edward and Alex Van Halen also do the same. And, as it just so happens, the similarity doesn't end there. "After Vinnie had been playing for about a year, I hopped on his kit and tried to hang with him, but he just totally blew me away," Dime reveals. "Our story is almost identical to the Van Halen one, I guess. Both Eddie and Alex played drums, but Alex killed and so Eddie decided to pick up the guitar. It was the same thing in our case. Riggs (Vinnie's nickname) definitely dominated me on the kit, so I started playing guitar.

"Vinnie taught me a lot about timing," Darrell continues. "For example, I can remember one day we were jamming around together and decided that we were gonna try to learn 'More Than a Feeling' by Boston. We started dicking with it right before we had to leave for school, and we were already late when Vinnie pointed out that I was leaving out one chord—that I was coming outta one section before the drum beat had a chance to turn around. I was like, 'What are you talking about?' So he counted everything out for me and showed me where I was missing the chord. Then we went back and listened to the record and, sure enough, he was right.

"It's always been like that with us. Vinnie is very knowledgeable and learned all his drum rudiments. He was the one who always paid attention in school! He's always had the business sense while I've had the street-level sense, and we work real well together, especially since we're both aiming for the same goals. I'm real fortunate to have a brother that I get on so well with and can rip on the drums like Vinnie can. I mean, it's hard enough to just find someone who can just beat on the skins in time."

In addition to being a monster drummer, Vinnie has another talent that has definitely contributed to Pantera's success. "Vinnie is the guy that followed in my old man's footsteps in the recording studio right off the bat," the guitarist points out. "He's a complete gear and gadget hound and really knows his way around a studio. In fact, Vinnie is partly responsible for my recorded sound.

"On our early demos [which were recorded and produced by Dime's father, Jerry Abbott, who was often credited on the sleeve as "The Eld'n"] I was really frustrated with my recorded sound. I'd say to my dad, 'I need more cut on my guitar; I want more treble.' He just didn't understand what I was getting at so he'd just say, 'No, son, you don't want that—it'll hurt your ears.' It wasn't until Vinnie started getting behind the mixing board that things started to sound the way I wanted them to sound."

Camp Strapped
Although Dime is quick to pay kudos to his brother's skills in the studio, he is no slouch with recording gear himself. His current home in Arlington, Texas, an eccentric dwelling lovingly named Camp Strapped, houses a pretty impressive recording studio in the garage at the bottom of his backyard. Dime's initial intention was merely to build a home-based jam room/demo studio, but when Pantera did some recording down there prior to making *The Great Southern Trendkill* in 1997, that plan changed. "Everyone was really digging the sound we were getting in my jam room, so we decided to do the recording right there," Dime explains. "I gotta tell you, man, those original demos were ****in' lethal—they sounded real tough and that was the deciding factor right there."

So, the band upgraded Dime's Camp Strapped studio and both *Trendkill* and *Reinventing the Steel* were recorded there. "It's pretty damned difficult to keep your dick hard on a song when you have to drive for 45 minutes to some alienating recording facility before can start jamming on it with your band," Darrell laughs. "And when you get there, you have to chill out and wait for everybody else to roll up. Then, of course, somebody's bound to be hungry so you leave the studio to go eat! This leaves you feeling like shit when you get back, and you end up slamming some beers and lying around watching a TV show you're not even interested in because your flame's not hot. And all the time you're waiting around to get inspired, you're shelling out big bucks for the place. To hell with that, man! We can do all time wasting stuff at my hut and it doesn't cost us a dime. We've got a keg going, 50 bottles of whiskey, a pool table, a big-screen TV—inspiration can and does strike at any moment, and it's easy to keep the fire going when all you've gotta do is walk to the bottom of the goddamned garden!"

The Four-Track King
In addition to the state-of-the-art 48-track facility at the bottom of his garden, Dime also has an eight-track setup upstairs that's always ready to roll. "That way, if I wake up in the middle of the night with a riff or some other idea in my head, I can just plug in and roll tape," the guitarist states. "Then I can crash back out, wake up later, listen to it

and, if it's any good, work on the idea some more." And then, of course, there's his all-time favorite piece of recording gear, the good ol' four-track.

"I'm the four-track king!" Dime roars. "I've pretty much always got a four-track with me and, on the rare occasions I don't, there's always my pocket recorder or the video camera. You never know when a riff idea is gonna come your way, so I try to always be prepared to capture them. I've learned the hard way that when you get a killer idea and you go, 'I'll remember that,' and start messing with it later on, it just ain't the same. You gotta get it on tape right away.

"I can't recommend getting a four-track enough, man. I've used mine every damned day since I got it. It's a total release, and the funny thing is, when you're dicking around with no real pressure, that's when you invariably hit gold. When a riff is written like that, it's definitely in its purest form 'cos it just came out naturally—you weren't sitting around waiting to be creative. That's why I keep going back and extracting riffs from my old four-track tapes. I mean, 'Shedding Skin' [*Far Beyond Driven*] is a four-track from like 40 years ago. Man, I've got thousands of songs I've done on my four-track—some are humorous and some are serious. If my liver don't give out on me, then maybe I'll get around to putting some of my four-track stuff out there to show some of the other sides of my playing."

Vulgar Display of Video
In addition to being a dab hand at audio recording, Dime is no slouch when it comes to capturing weird 'n' wonderful stuff on his video camera. In fact, he and the band's assistant/video sharkman Daryl "Bobby" Arnberger are responsible for filming and splicing together Pantera's three Gold-certified "home" videos: *Cowboys From Hell: The Videos*; *Vulgar Video*; and *Pantera 3: Watch It Go*. And, if you've seen 'em, you'll know that they're every bit as hardcore as you'd expect a Pantera video to be. "They just show what we do when we're on the road, man," laughs Dime. "We drink, we get drunk, we break stuff, we party, we gamble, we raise hell and we make a lot of people happy. So why not show the rest of the world? We put everything in there too. I'm sure most other bands would probably go, 'Hell, we can't show that,' but we don't give a damn. We work hard, we kick ass and we have fun too.

Interesting and inspirational stuff I'm sure you'll agree. However, we've managed to wander a tad off course here! So, let's return to the plot by turning the clock back to the early '80s.

A Band Is Born
Not surprisingly, the two teenage Abbott brother's decided to form a band together. So, in 1981, Pantera [the Spanish word for *panther*] was born. At the time, Vinnie was 17 while Dime was merely 15. They were joined by bassist Rex Rocker [full name Rex Brown] and vocalist Terry Lee Glaze. They cut their teeth on the local club circuit playing covers of their favorite metal acts of the era, namely Kiss, Van Halen, Ozzy Osbourne, Mötley Crüe, Metallica, Judas Priest, and the like. How good were they? If the fact that they were playing three one-hour sets a night seven days a week is anything to go by, they were exceptional!

In addition to sharpening their chops, both as individual players and as a band, Dime and Co.'s grueling nightclub gigging schedule also taught them how to drink! "We grew up in the clubs, man, and that was just part of the scene, y'know," the axeman explains. "It was all part of making it through the night! When you're playing three one-hour sets a night seven days a week month after month after month, the only things you've got are you, your axe, your band, the P.A. and your friends. And, in Texas, if you're kicking ass up there on that stage, people send you shots to show their appreciation. So, what do you do? Turn the shot down and piss off some big-assed dude and his buds! [laughs]. Not in Texas, bro! You grab the thing, say 'thanks,' down the thing and go with it. We've always said that our time playing clubs developed our playing *and* our drinking chops!"

Metal Magic
In addition to turning out killer covers, the band started to write their own material. And, by 1983, they'd amassed enough songs and earned a big enough local following for an album to be warranted. So, they formed their own label, Metal Magic Records & Tapes and, with Dime's and Vinnie's father at the production helm, Pantera's debut album, *Metal Magic*, was born. The ten songs it contained were typical of the metal of the day—melodic and thickly laden with vocal harmonies. This said, Dime's hard-hitting guitar work and the impressive tightness of the rhythm section formed by Vinnie and Rex made it clear that the band could kick butt with the best of them.

Metal fanzines the world over were quick to pour critical praise on the album and, as a result, *Metal Magic* was soon picked up for widespread distribution and found its way into all the specialty record stores that mattered. Not surprisingly, the boys were quick to write and record their sophomore LP.

Seek...It Destroys!

Pantera's second self-released album, *Projects in the Jungle*, hit the streets in 1984 and, in my humble opinion, is a rare gem that is well worth tracking down if you're a serious fan of Dimebag's playing. Despite the fact that: 1) the album's artwork is, to put it politely, rather dodgy, and 2) the relative lightness of the songs will probably leave modern-day Pantera fans scratching their heads in bewilderment, it truly is a great record. Plus, the fretblazing antics of the then 19-year-old Dime are both brilliant and breathtaking.

Don't believe me? Then check out what the British magazine *Kerrang!* had to say: "[*Projects in the Jungle*] remains a monster record. It might sound amusing to latter-day fans, but it stood head and shoulders above most records released in 1984. Heavier than the debut, in a Def Leppard-meets-Van Halen sense, the Abbott brothers seemed to be in competition as to who could go the most over-the-top in the playing stakes. Add to this Rex's booming bass lines, Terry Glaze's screaming to the heavens and the inclusion of a song titled 'Heavy Metal Rules,' and you've got a classic release." Coming from the publication that is considered by many to be the bible of heavy metal, this is praise indeed!

I Am the Night

A year later, Pantera's third self-released album, *I Am the Night*, emerged and was well received by both fans and critics alike. Once again, *Kerrang!* championed the release with a rave review that included the following: "technical and mental advances in all areas have teased the songs and the performances into kaleidoscopic instances of raw power." While agreeing wholeheartedly that Dime, Vinnie and Rex deserved such praise, at the risk of sounding cruel, it has to be said that *I Am the Night* made it pretty darned clear that vocalist Terry Glaze was struggling to keep up—and failing. Dime and Co. clearly were aiming for heavier, harder, faster ground, and their singer's David Lee Roth-like pop/rock approach just wasn't working anymore. The band started to notice this and so did their fans.

Ch, Ch, Ch, Changes

"We used to play at a club in Shreveport, Louisiana, and every time we did a show down there, people would tell us that our lead singer wasn't cutting it and that we should check out a guy named Phil who sang in Razor White," Vinnie Paul recounted while taking a break from mastering *Reinventing the Steel*. "Apparently, the same people used to tell Phil that Pantera needed a new singer and that he should join. He called me up one day and we shot the shit for about an hour. Man, as soon as I hung up with him, I called up Dime and said, 'Dude, I've found our new singer,' I swear to God, Phil was the most charismatic guy I'd ever spoken to—I felt like I'd just been on the phone with Paul Stanley!

"We brought him up to Texas for an audition, and it just clicked into place right away," the amiable drummer continues. "Phil was a total godsend—honest, real and one hell of a singer and frontman. He went home, quit his band, packed up his shit and relocated to Texas. At the risk of sounding corny, Phil was the missing piece of the Pantera jigsaw puzzle. Getting him in the band enabled us all to totally focus and move forward in the direction we always wanted to go in."

Historical Note 1: Just so you trivia-buffs know, Terry Glaze and Pantera actually parted company some time prior to Phil Anselmo joining the band's ranks. The reason? That good old (but in this case true) "musical differences" chestnut. A Houston-based dude with the rather un-metal name of Matt L'Amour was announced as the band's new frontman when Glaze departed but was gone in a heartbeat, as was his replacement, David Peacock. Got it? Good! Let's get back to the meat of the story.

Rebirth and Power Metal

To say that the recruitment of 18-year-old Phil Anselmo breathed new live into Pantera's already vibrant being would be one of the grossest understatements of all time. He didn't make his recording debut with the band until a good year-and-a-half had passed, but the wait was well worth it. Enter the band's fourth self-released opus, *Power Metal*, in 1988. This, my friends, is a barnstorming '80s metal album of which, I'm convinced, even the almighty Judas Priest would've been proud to have spawned. With the notable exception of the rather Keel-like (surprise, surprise!) Marc Ferrari-penned "Proud to Be Loud" (even Dime's ripping lead break couldn't salvage this one!), this album shines from start to finish. The whole band perform like men possessed—both as a unit and as individuals—none more so than

Dime, whose lead work is outstanding throughout. As was the case with *Projects in the Jungle*, if you're a diehard Darrell fan, this hard-to-find LP is a must-have item. Hell, it's worth tracking down purely to find out what on earth "P?S?T?88" is all about!

To get a true indication of the new level of confidence and power Anselmo added to Pantera, compare the version of "Down Below" that appears on *Power Metal* with the one on *I Am the Night*. Can you say, "night and day"? As Dime would no doubt explain, "It's like the difference between nonalcoholic beer and real beer!"

Historical Note 2: Yep, it's time for more trivia. In case you're wondering why a band of Pantera's obvious songwriting talent would record a song penned by Marc Ferrari of the '80s band Keel, read on. Thanks to a strong recommendation from Mr. Ferrari, Pantera landed a deal with Gold Mountain Records, a label distributed by the mighty Atlantic Records. When Atlantic heard the album, however, they felt it was too heavy for their liking (they were expecting a more Bon Jovi-like vibe apparently!), and so Gold Mountain gave Pantera the rights to release *Power Metal* and eventually let the band go altogether—the fools! What makes this story even more amusing/ironic is the fact that Atco, the label that signed a much heavier Dime and Co. a mere two years later, was also a subsidiary of Atlantic!

Looks That Kill?

As certain facets of the metal press have taken great delight in pointing out by printing old pictures, from *Metal Magic* ('83) to their *Power Metal* period ('88/'89), Pantera looked like a typical '80s glam metal band—from the spandex pants right through to the obligatory big hair. In keeping with their patented no-bullshit approach to all things Pantera, Dime and Co. neither deny nor dismiss this period of their existence. Over, once again, to the ever-eloquent Vinnie Paul:

"That was what metal was back then," the drummer states. "We were playing the club circuit, covering all our favorite songs by Van Halen, Judas Priest, Mötley Crüe, etc., and that's the way metal bands looked at that time. I mean, look at Ozzy during his *The Ultimate Sin* period—jeez, you can even dig up old pictures of James Hetfield [Metallica] wearing spandex. It's just that our old shots have gotten more publicity. Take a look at a picture of yourself from ten years ago and you'll realize that you've changed. What we looked like in the '80s was merely what was going on back then, that's all. Of all people, Phil will bust out one of our old LPs and say, 'This shit kicks ass!' And it did; they were good albums for their time."

Well said, Riggs! Case closed. Needless to say, when the band's next album, the crushing *Cowboys From Hell*, was unleashed in 1990, the fearsome foursome's image was the scruffy street urchin one we now know and love. As *CFH* signaled the start of the much (much!) better-known period of the band's career thus far, I'm gonna revert to a much briefer form of synopsis from here on in.

1989: Dime is offered the chance to fill the vacant lead-guitarist slot in one of the biggest metal bands of all time, Megadeth. Much to the chagrin of Megadeth's main man Dave Mustaine, however, Darrell politely turns it down—such was the strength of his commitment to Pantera! A few years later, while touring in support of *Vulgar Display of Power*, Pantera opened up for Megadeth in Europe, so clearly Dime's loyalty didn't cause an unbridgeable rift between the two acts.

1990: Thanks to the underground success of *Power Metal* and Pantera's fast-growing reputation as an unstoppable live act, the band sign a deal with major label, Atco, and the *Cowboys From Hell* album is released. The boys then hit the road with a vengeance—a place they'll stay for the next eight years or so, pausing only to write and record a new album.

1991: After 180+ shows, including a stint in Europe opening for one of their all-time favorite bands, Judas Priest, the "Cowboys From Hell" tour finally ends. *Cowboys From Hell: The Videos* is released and the band heads back into the studio to record their next album. The LP is completed in a short two months and then the band flies to Russia to play for more than 750,000 people at the "Monsters of Rock" show in Moscow. Also on the bill is Metallica, AC/DC and the Black Crowes. "I dunno what was more amazing about that gig—the number of fans there or the dudes we played with!" Dime stated afterward.

1992: *Vulgar Display of Power* is released and earns the band their first-ever appearance on the U.S. Billboard charts, entering at #42. The band immediately hits the road again, opening for, of all people, Skid Row! The tour is a huge success. The readership of *Guitar for the Practicing Musician* recognize Dime's huge potential by voting him Best Breakthrough Guitarist in the publication's Readers' Poll '92.

1993: The band continues to tour the world like men possessed and end up staying on the road for a staggering 287 days. Their second long-form video, *Vulgar Video*, is released and, like its predecessor, *Cowboys From Hell: The Videos*, goes Gold in America. *Vulgar Display of Power* deservedly becomes Pantera's first album to achieve Gold status (500,000 sales) in America and eventually goes Platinum (1,000,000 sales) in the U.S., U.K., Australia, Canada and Japan. As soon as the tour is finished, Dime and Co. head straight for the studio to commence work on the next LP.

1994: Pantera's third major-label album, the aptly named *Far Beyond Driven*, is written and recorded in a staggering six weeks and unleashed on the eagerly awaiting public. The LP sells like those proverbial hotcakes and on March 21, 1994, makes history by becoming the first-ever heavy metal album to debut at #1 in America! As is now the norm, the band immediately hits the touring trail again, circling the globe, selling out arenas and leaving a trail of destruction and delighted fans behind. The tour includes a triumphant appearance in front of 72,000 fans at the prestigious Monsters of Rock festival in Donnington, England.

1995: More touring! Also, "I'm Broken" (*Far Beyond Driven*) is deservedly nominated for the Best Metal Performance Grammy. Sadly, it doesn't win. As a consolation though, Dime and Pantera do rather well in *Guitar World's* 1995 Readers' Poll: Darrell is voted Best Heavy Metal Guitarist and comes in second (behind Eric Clapton) in the Most Valuable Player category. Also, his "Planet Caravan" lead wins the Best Solo category, and *Far Beyond Driven* is voted the Best Heavy Metal Album. Darrell is also voted Best Metal Guitarist by the readership of *Guitar Player* magazine in its annual poll.

1996: The band's eagerly awaited next album, *The Great Southern Trendkill*, is released and proves to be the most brutal album of the year, bar none. Pantera does a co-headlining U.S. summer tour with White Zombie, which proves to be one of the few stadium-filling successes of the year. The band then heads for Japan, Australia and New Zealand where, as always, they leave rubble in their wake.

In July though, tragedy nearly strikes when vocalist Philip Anselmo collapses after a show in Dallas. It turns out he had overdosed on heroin and actually died for a few minutes. "There were no lights, no beautiful music, just nothing," the singer revealed in a statement he issued shortly afterward. Thankfully, Philip made a quick and full recovery.

Dime is voted Best Hard Rock/Heavy Metal Guitarist in the *Guitar World* Readers' Poll and Best Metal Guitarist in *Guitar Player* magazine's poll.

1997: Pantera starts off the year with a bang by opening up for their boyhood idols, Kiss, on a tour of South America. "We played in front of 50,000–100,000 people every night," Dime smiles. "It was an unbelievable experience, a dream come true. I always figured that playing a gig with the original Kiss line-up would be the all-time topper, and it was! We would have done it for free!"

The band's *Official Live: 101 Proof* is released in July and features two new studio cuts, "Where You Come From" and "I Can't Hide," in addition to blistering live performances of 12 Pantera classics. The band then heads straight back out on the road on Ozzfest '97, a summer tour of America that includes the reformed Black Sabbath (minus drummer Bill Ward) and Marilyn Manson. As always, they crush.

"Suicide Note Part 1" is nominated for the Best Metal Performance Grammy but doesn't win. Then, to top off yet another hectic year, in the fall the band releases their third home video, *3: Watch It Go*, which entered the Billboard video charts at #1. Just like its two predecessors, Dime's latest piece of video "art" quickly achieves Gold status. Last, but definitely not least, Dime is once again voted Best Hard Rock/Metal Guitarist by the readers of *Guitar World*. And, if that's not enough, he also wins the Most Valuable Player (M.V.P.) category in the poll! The readers of *Guitar Magazine* also vote him Best Rock Guitarist.

1998: The band continues touring, including a show-stealing slot at the Milton Keynes, England date of Ozzfest '98. They then take a short but well-earned break (their first in nearly eight years) before commencing work on their eagerly awaited next studio album. The band gets their second Best Metal Performance Grammy nomination for the live version of "Cemetary Gates" that appears on *Official Live: 101 Proof*. Unfortunately, yet again, they don't win. So much for that old saying, "Third time lucky."

To cap off another fine year for the band, Dime once again wins the Best Hard Rock/Metal Guitarist category in *Guitar World's* Annual Readers' Poll, making it the fourth consecutive year he's won the award.

1999: Work on the next album is interrupted when their icons, Black Sabbath, personally invite Pantera to open for them on their hugely successful Reunion tour of America (with Bill Ward!). "Touring with Sabbath was one of the greatest thrills of my life," Darrell gushes. "Watching them play every night and having the chance to hang out with those guys was unbelievable. Tony [Iommi] even let me dye his goatee purple one time!"

The quartet also finds time to open for Metallica in Mexico and provokes a riot with their first crushing chord. "It was just a sea of chairs, man!" Dime recalls. Somehow, in between all of this roadwork, the boys manage to continue working on their pending record.

2000: The editors of *Guitar One* magazine hail Dimebag as an M.V.P. and dub him "the progenitor of the modern metal sound, with chops to boot." *Reinventing the Steel* is released to a tidal wave of critical acclaim and public embrace. It enters the U.S. album charts at #4. The band kicks off its world tour by conquering Europe and Japan before returning to the U.S. to dominate Ozzfest 2000.

Reinventing the Steel is certified Gold in the U.S. and Dime returns to penning his monthly "Riffer Madness" column in *Guitar World* magazine, much to the delight of his countless fans.

2001: Pantera gets fourth Grammy nomination as "Revolution Is My Name" is named as one of the contenders in the Best Metal Performance category. Adding to the honors being heeped on the band, Dime gets voted Best Metal Guitarist (yet again!) and *Reinventing the Steel* wins Best Metal Guitar Album of 2000 in *Guitar World* magazine's 2001 Readers' Poll. And, talking of readers' polls—Pantera pulled off a clean sweep in *Metal Edge* magazine's 16th Annual Reader's Choice Awards by winning the Band of the Year, Guitarist of the Year, Album of the Year, Album Cover of the Year, Song of the Year, Vocalist of the Year, Drummer of the Year and Bassist of the Year categories!

After a lengthy U.S. headlining tour, including three sold-out New York shows, Pantera hook up with their old pals Slayer and continue crushing the States that summer on the aptly named and highly successful "Extreme Steel" trek. Sadly, the rest of the world misses out on this deadly duo when the unspeakable terrorist acts of 9/11 prevent Pantera from spearheading the highly anticipated "Tattoo the Planet" tour with Kerry King & Co.

To be continued. May Pantera truly "grind that axe for a long time!"

"We're four guys who are like family—we're in love with what we do and we're on fire when we're touring, man. We ain't never gonna stop— we'll be the Rolling Stones of the heavy shit!"

Dimebag Darrell

FOOTNOTE: What's in a Name?

As you may have noticed, Darrell Lance Abbott has used more than one name during his tenure in Pantera, the only band he's ever been in. Here's a quick recap: On 1983's *Metal Magic*, his name appeared on the album sleeve simply as Darrell Abbott. When *Power Metal* hit the shelves in '88, however, he'd replaced his surname with his middle name and was listed as Darrell Lance. Then, on *Cowboys From Hell* and *Vulgar Display of Power*, he became Diamond Darrell before morphing seamlessly into his most infamous nickname of all, Dimebag Darrell. "My friends have called me Dimebag for as long as I can remember," Darrell reveals. "Diamond was my nickname to begin with, and then they started to call me Dimebag because that's all I could ever afford! I've also been called Dime, Five & Dime and even Desmond—whatever you want it to be. That's just something we do down south, man. We're big on nicknames. That way, when you can't remember some dude's name, you just give him a new one!"

Chapter 3

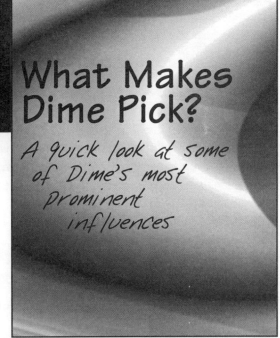

What Makes Dime Pick?

A quick look at some of Dime's most prominent influences

It's a well-known fact that one of the best ways of getting a true handle on what makes a particular guitar player play the way he or she does is by taking a look at his or her influences. So, let's do exactly that with Dime.

Although his top three are **Edward Van Halen, Randy Rhoads** and **Ace Frehley,** what you're about to read is quite a list of players. Why? 'Goddamn, brother, if you love listening to guitar playing as much as I do, then there's no way you're gonna answer that question with just one or two names. There are millions of great ones!" Dime explains.

So, in keeping with Darrell's feelings on this subject, below is a pretty comprehensive list of his biggest influences, both past and present. The top three are tackled first and then the rest of the usual suspects follow in no particular order. And, as I'm sure you'll be delighted to read, each one features some insightful comments from the Dimester himself.

Randy Rhoads

"Randy Rhoads was a killer lead player, and his riffs were unbelievable—every song was full of them. I mean the first time I heard the intro to "Crazy Train" I was like, "Goddamn, I gotta learn this!" I was crashed out hard in my bed, definitely not wanting to go to school, then Vinnie came in and cranked that sucker up. Man, that song busted me in the ass so damned hard I had to get up! I think I stayed off school for three days straight trying to learn that opening riff!

"I loved Randy's brittle sound and his awesome ability to double his leads—the 'Crazy Train' solo really shows how well he did that. I double my leads sometimes and that's something I definitely learned from him—especially the way he played them. He'd do the double tight but loose, so they'd flange together just a little. That's what I try to do on solos like the one I do in 'I'm Broken' [Far Beyond Driven: See Chapter 9 for a note-for-note breakdown of this solo].

"Y'know, I can't say enough good things about Randy and the influence he's had on me, especially when it comes to orchestrating shit. The classical vibe he had was incredible. I mean, 'Revolution Mother Earth' off the first Randy Rhoads 'n' Ozzy record [Blizzard of Ozz] is like Beethoven to me! The way he mixed classical style playing with chunky, metal riffs was incredible.

"I dig all of Randy's solos, but right here, right now though, the solo he did in 'Revelation Mother Earth' is ringing out pretty hard as my all-time favorite—that'll probably change in a few minutes though! Anyways, the whole structure behind that solo is real cool and I love that mode he plays it in—that Egyptian-sounding shit or whatever it is. The solo just takes off and burns, then ends with a killer melody before going 'wrrrr' right into 'Steal Away the Night.' I thought that was totally ****in' bad-assed the very first time I heard it and still do to this very day. There's no telling what that cat would be bustin' off if he was still around. He was a monster player and his guitar work on Blizzard of Ozz and Diary of a Madman was definitely one step above anything else going on at that time. To me, Eddie Van Halen was heavy rock 'n' roll, but Randy was heavy metal."

Eddie Van Halen

"Eddie is definitely the breakthrough guitarist of the last 20 years, and his innovative style, originality, heartfelt playing, pure energy and fire let me know that what you could do on the guitar is unlimited. I was a little kid when I first heard *Van Halen I*, and I just couldn't believe what I was hearing. Eddie just rips the strings off his guitar and plays with such a fierce aggression. His guitar sound was unbeatable too. There was a time in the '80s when every town in America had someone who'd play 'Eruption' note for note. Well, in Texas I was that dude! When we were playing the clubs in the early days, I always played 'Eruption' in my solo. I always ****ed up the ending though!

"Eddie was a huge influence on me without a doubt. His raw spontaneity always lights me up. He made me look at the instrument in a different way, man. He made me look at it as a tool you can screw around with rather than something you should always play very carefully and precisely. He proved technical playing can still be aggressive. I still listen to the first two Van Halen albums all the time; they're both ****in' on fire and still kick my ass!"

Ace Frehley and Kiss

Ace is God and I always get all wound-up talking about Kiss because *Alive!* is what turned me on to hard rock. That album influenced me to go out and buy other heavy records by bands like Black Sabbath and Judas Priest. It definitely changed my life and led me down the right path, brother! Plus it's front-to-back with killer songs.

"I'm a huge fan of Ace's playing, and his solo album [*Ace Frehley*] is one of my all time favorites—you can find it being played on my juke box all the time. Every song's a great one and every solo shines. His vibrato is what really grabbed me at first 'cos he could squeeze so much out of a single note—he can definitely make that one note take the place of twelve. He also has a great tone and a very distinctive playing style, but it's not flashy or tricky. It's just raw, straight-up, bad-assed guitar-playing.

"Although Eddie and Randy were both massive influences on me, Ace Frehley was probably my biggest one of all. He's actually the reason I started playing guitar. I got a fake Les Paul and I used to skip school, go home and dress up like him—it just all went from there. Hell, I've even got a signed tattoo of Ace on my chest, man. That's how much I think of him—he's always gonna be with me."

Glen Tipton and K.K. Downing of Judas Priest

"As far as I'm concerned, Glen and K.K. are the gods of double-guitar axemanship. They both have great tone and totally unique styles and are real band-orientated players. They're also both tremendously underrated. Priest's *British Steel* album is one of the greatest metal albums of all time, and it totally rearranged my way of thinking. It's the full-meal deal—its got bad-assed songwriting, bad-assed singing, bad-assed rhythms, bad-assed lead and a totally brutal sound. Today's music can't touch it. That album is why I have a razor blade around my neck [the cover of *British Steel* has a picture of a fist gripping a razor blade]. My chick got me that necklace and I've worn it forever. A lot of people think it's for cocaine or crank but it ain't. I've drunk millions of gallons of whisky and beer in my time, but I don't touch that stuff."

Ty Tabor of King's X

"There's just something about Ty Tabor's style—his tone and honest feel—that kills me every time. And the same goes for [King's X's vocalist/bassist] Doug Pinnick—his bass tone, his vocal melodies, harmonies and songs—the whole thing just gets it for me in many, many ways. I ****in' love King's X. Doug recently gave me a copy of their latest album [*Please Come Home...Mr. Bulbous*] and it's pure bliss to me."

Dave Murray and Adrian Smith of Iron Maiden

"Both those guys are bad-assed players who could shred with the best when they wanted but would hang back and play choice notes too. They did killer dual-guitar playing, and both had great tones for rhythm and lead. *The Number of the Beast* album is just a straight-up, kick-ass metal album that is 100% solid from start to finish. It's full of great songs and brutal sounds."

Scott Ian and Anthrax

"I was only a kid when they came out with *Spreading the Disease*, and it totally blew me away. Scott's rhythm sound hit me like someone had smashed me in the face with a 2 x 4, and what [drummer] Charlie Benante was doing with his feet on songs like 'Gung Ho' really was the shit. Their next album, *Among the Living*, also got me going pretty ***in' hard."

Bugs Henderson

"He puts his whole heart into it and he's an honest blues player. I guess you could say he was an early influence on me seeing as he recorded at my dad's studio. I'd go down while he was recording and the dude was cool enough to let me hang around and watch him play."

James Hetfield of Metallica

"Metallica's a huge influence on us all, and their old albums lit one hell of a fire under my ass! James Hetfield is truly phenomenal, man—he's the god of the chugging, metal riff. I don't know of any guitarist who can down-pick like James can. I know I sure as hell can't! I mean, check out a song like 'Motorbreath' [*Kill 'em All*]; that's a prime example of his awesome expertise in this area. It's real heavy but real clean—I definitely learned how to play clean, driving rhythms from that song. To me, *Kill 'em All* is full of unbelievable riffs, and every song cuts like a razor blade. It never fails to get me motivated, and we'll still put it on backstage to get us fired-up before a show. *Master of Puppets* still beats me down in the dirt too."

Tony Iommi of Black Sabbath

"What can you say about the dude who's the god of the heavy metal riff? He's written a shitload of classic stuff and it'll still be considered classic in 50 years' time. Like I just told you, getting into Kiss was my first real rock 'n' roll experience, and I thought they were about as heavy as it could get. Then, when I was about 13, I heard "Iron Man" and it blew my ****in' mind—it was so powerful and heavy. I've been a huge Sabbath fan ever since. Man, the intro riff to 'Into the Void' [*Master of Reality*] may well be the heaviest thing I've ever heard—it still gets my dick hard three or four times a day!

"Tony has a monstrous sound and he also has a frantic, skidding vibrato technique that's totally killer. He started all that de-tuning shit, and he's a solid, chunky rhythm player too. I really respect the fact that he concentrates on rhythm rather than lead—he's always looking at the big picture and doing what's appropriate for the song. That's something I try to do in my playing too."

David Allan Coe (a country music institution most famous for penning the '70s hit "Take This Job and Shove It")

"Man, I've been a fan of his for as long as I've been walking! He is to country-and-western what we are to heavy metal. I've come to find that almost everybody loves this country-punk legend, even cats like Kid Rock. I went to see him play a while ago and I gave him a copy of our third home video, *3: Watch It Go*. I said, 'Hey, man, you probably ain't heard of us but that don't matter none. Here's what we do, we're pretty much like you in as much as we're both rebels.' We ended up shooting the shit for two hours backstage and found we had a bunch of stuff in common. Anyways, he called me up a couple of days later and said, 'Hey, Dime, it's David Allan Coe. I'm gambling and I just hit $50,000 in a slot machine! I want you to play on my next record.' He had a week off so I invited him up to my place to stay. We shot a lot of whiskey, and him, me, Riggs and Rex started cutting shit together for a crossover project called "David Allen Coe and the Cowboys From Hell." We'll probably name the album *Rebel Meets Rebel* when it's done.

"Collaborating with a country legend like him is cool. I love the fact that he's an outlaw and goes against the grain by opening his shows by doing Pantera tunes and shit like that. He's totally on top of what's going on too, man—he reads more rock magazines and owns more rock albums than most kids I know."

Billy Gibbons of ZZ Top

"We're all huge ZZ Top fans. I'm not a super blues player or anything, but I grew up surrounded by that Texas blues stuff and some of it has definitely rubbed off on me. To me, blues is all about feel, vibe and tone, and Billy definitely has all that goin' on. Check out a song like "Tush" [*Fandango*]. Man, I love the way he'll let one note ring out until it dies away and then gets that rattling noise of the string rubbing on the frets. A bunch of the little things I do like that I got from listening to the Reverend Billy G!

"I dig all of Billy's stuff, but *Degullo* is probably my favorite ZZ album because of his bluesy, heavy feel on it. You don't ever think of ZZ Top as a metal band, but there are some *heavy* jams on that album. Whenever I listen to him, he takes me away from play 5,000 notes, especially when he gets hold of one and squeezes it from his soul. To me a genuine sound travels to your fingers from the soul."

Blues Saraceno

"Man, I could listen to that cat all day long. His *Plaid* and *Never Look Back* albums rule—he's killer, man. Blues never overplays, and his feel is so honest. His tone is killer too, and you can always tell it's him. That dude is everything that guitar stands for. I've even got a little green plaid tattoo on my leg 'cos of Blues—that's how much I think of him."

Kerry King and Jeff Hanneman of Slayer

"Damn! What can you say about those two guys, man? They both have a real unorthodox playing style that's definitely NOT normal. They have unbelievable rhythm chops too, and they play with real guts and aggression. It almost sounds like they make up their own ****in' scales, and they definitely do nothing by the book, but it never sounds out of place! Listening to those dudes taught me how to play with guts and aggression.

"Those dudes have always stayed true to their guns and, as a call out to them, there's a line in 'Goddamn Electric' [*Reinventing the Steel*] that goes, 'Your trust is in whiskey and weed and Slayer, it's goddamn electric." So, when Slayer played the Dallas Starplex on the [1999] Ozzfest, we asked Kerry if he'd play the outro solo on it. He went, 'Sure, man' so we took a bunch of recording gear down and set it up in this tiny bathroom backstage. Then, as soon as Kerry was done jamming on stage, he rolled in one of his Marshall stacks and let rip. The first thing he played was so awesome I yelled, 'That's it! That's the one! Don't touch it!' God knows what the hell he did, but goddamn, he pulls some shit off. That's one hell of a bad-assed lead!"

Jimmy Page

"I woke up to Led Zeppelin only a few years back, man. When I was a kid I never got it—I never heard all the cool feel and guitar layering things he had doing. I definitely get it now though. Led Zeppelin is a bad-assed band, and as soon as the penny dropped I went out and bought their entire catalogue. Man, what a totally killer experience that was—it was like having a favorite band and not having to wait for them to put any records out! You can never play a Jimmy Page riff and get it to sound exactly the way it sounds on record 'cos of his symphonic layering of parts."

Pete Willis of Def Leppard

"The first Def Leppard album, *On Through the Night*, is a killer album, and their original guitarist Pete Willis was a great player. He really inspired me early on because I was a small, young dude and he was one too—and he was out there kickin' some serious ass. He definitely made me wanna get out there and do the same exact thing."

Angus Young of AC/DC

"I can't say enough good shit about his playing 'cos he really stands out from other players. He has a unique tone and a totally killer vibrato technique. He plays totally clean, too, like he's playing on a Marshall turned up to 12 without the gain control cranked—it's pure output distortion, not preamp or stomp-box fuzz."

Rusty Johnson (ex-Point Blank) of Big Foot Johnson

This dude plays around town [Dallas] and he's brought a lot of joy to my heart in the guitar realm. He used to be in a band called Point Blank that had some big hits back in the late '70s/early '80s. Y'know, a lot of people give up after they have their big rush or whatever, but this dude is one dude that never quit and won't quit either—he just keeps coming with it. You should hear what this cat plays, man! He plays left-handed on a right-handed guitar strung-up for a righty; it's bizarre to watch. I don't have to pay no $17.50 to go see him either—I can catch him right up the street at the bar and he never misses a note. I just sit there, drink and go, 'What the ****!' Anyway, he's definitely had an influence on me lately, man—somebody who's already topped everything and just keeps topping it. He's in the forty-something category now but he don't show it, man. He aims to kill every time he plays, and it reminds me what it's all about."

Metal of Honor

Other metal/hard rock guitarists and bands Dime has mentioned as being influential/inspirational include Accept (particularly the *Balls to the Wall* album); Jerry Cantrell of Alice in Chains ("He plays his ass off on *Dirt*"); Motorhead; the Scorpions (especially the *Lovedrive* LP); Pat Travers and Pat Thrall of the Pat Travers Band (especially the live album, *Go for What You Know*); Michael Schenker; and Robin Trower.

None More Metal

Also, the fact that Dime has already mentioned players like Billy Gibbons and country legend David Allan Coe proves that although he's a true metal head, he does listen to other forms of music! "I've always liked a lot of country stuff 'cos I grew up around it in my dad's studio," Darrell confesses. "I mean, Merle Haggard's shit is killer. I'm a huge, huge fan of [Lynyrd] Skynyrd too, man, and who the hell isn't? Dude, if you don't like that band, then there's something severely wrong with you! Believe it or not, I like Steely Dan too. Damn, I could go on about stuff I like that's not metal for hours and hours."

Chapter 4

The Tone Zone

Dime's axes, amps 'n' FX

"The guitar is a killer-sounding instrument. That's why we play it!"

Dimebag

Like all serious guitarists, Dime is fanatical about his sound and has spent countless hours fine-tuning it. As a direct result of his dedication, not only does Dime have a great tone, but he also has successfully achieved every axeman's dream: the creation of a signature sound that is instantly recognizable and often aped. So, in this chapter, we're gonna take a look at the gear he uses—from strings to speakers.

WARNING: Even if you duplicated Dime's rig exactly, the chances of you sounding exactly like him are far beyond slim. Hell, even if you were to play Dime's axe through Dime's rig, you probably wouldn't sound like him! Why? Well, although the gear being used will obviously have a definite bearing on how you sound (e.g., a Gibson Les Paul into a cranked Marshall stack will sound very different from a Fender Tele plugged into a Vox AC30 regardless of who's playing them!), ultimately the person who's actually playing has the biggest bearing of all—namely YOU! It's all down to hands 'n' heart, y'see! And that's a good thing, believe me! Jeez, if we all sounded the same, the guitar would lose most of its magic—to me, at any rate. And, ultimately, don't you wanna sound like yourself anyway!? Think about it.

If you like the way Dime sounds, then you're much better off plugging a guitar with a locking whammy system and a hot, humbucking pickup into a high-gain amp than you would be plugging a single-coil loaded Strat into a Fender Twin! As already stated though, just don't expect to instantly become Dime's doppelganger, even if you copy his set-up—a truth the man himself will reiterate later on. This said, let's get into Dime's gear. We're gonna do this in two stages:

1. By taking a quick tour through the gear he's used over the years, starting with *Cowboys From Hell* (1990) and noting how it's metamorphosed over the years.

2. By looking at a couple of *Riffer Madness* questions that were gear-related. And one of 'em has Dime giving us a no-holds-barred look at the very heart of the killer-sounding rig he was using during Pantera's *Far Beyond Driven* period (1994/5).

Got it? Good. Let's get to it.

Get a Grip: Dime's Picks
"When I play live, I jump around like an idiot for 90 minutes or more under a lighting rig that's hotter than hell," Dime states. "This makes me sweat like a pig, making it real tough for me to keep a firm grip on my picks, even those ones that are supposed to be non-slip. Losing control of your pick on stage sucks the big one, so I scratch some deep X's into both sides of 'em with something sharp, like a dart. Scratching grooves into your picks makes 'em look like shit, but at least you won't look like an asshole because you dropped one in the middle of a solo!" Dime has also been known to slice up the volume knobs on his guitars for the same exact reason, to make them sweat-proof.

Strings 'n' Things
As you'll soon discover in **Chapter 6**, for the vast majority of the time, Dime uses three tunings:
1. "Regular" concert pitch (low to high: E A D G B E)
2. "Drop D" (low to high: D A D G B E)
3. "Down a whole-step" (low to high: D G C F A D)

He's also used other tunings from time to time, like the "down one-and-a-half steps" (C♯ F♯ B E G♯ C♯) he uses on "Drag the Waters" [*The Great Southern Trendkill*] for example. Talking of tunings, as you'll discover in **Chapter 6**, Dime tunes "a C-hair flat" so his "A" doesn't equal 440 Hz.

Dime uses two different sets of string gauges, depending on his tuning. He uses (from high to low) .009, .011, .016, .026, .036 and .046 on his "regular" tuned axes and .009, .011, .016, .028, .038 and .050 on the rest. His string brand of choice? He used to use La Bella but nowadays he swears by DR strings.

Axes, Whammy Bar Systems and Pickups

In the same exact way Tony Iommi is immediately associated with an SG and Ace Frehley with a Les Paul, Dime's identity is inextricably linked with the shape of a Dean ML. For many years, Dime's main axe was his battered 'n' blue "lightning bolt" Dean ML (built in 1981, serial # 8103093), complete with "the Dean from Hell" written on the headstock and a Kiss sticker behind the bridge. This guitar was the one he won in a guitar contest when he was a teenager, and it quickly became his main axe. When he first got it though, it wasn't blue.

Lightning Strikes

"That axe has got a cool story behind it," smiles Dime. "My dad bought me my first Dean for Christmas 'cos I kept busting his ass for it. It cost him a lot of money, but he knew I was dying for one so he hooked me up. For that, I'll be forever grateful to him, man, 'cos I'd wanted one for years. When I was 13, y'see, I got a Dean catalogue and nearly dumped in my pants! I thought the ML was the baddest-looking guitar in the world. I loved its half Flying V, half Explorer vibe and its big-assed headstock."

Dime was understandably delighted with his dream Christmas present. Trouble was, less than two weeks later he won another Dean in a guitar playing contest, and it played and sounded better than his other one. "I was thrilled to have two Deans, but I was 16 and I really needed some wheels," Dime recalls. So as not to "bum out" his Dad, Dime did the honorable thing and sold the contest axe so he could buy a car.

The ML Dime sold, changed hands a few times and ended up with that respected Texan guitar builder/repair man Buddy Blaze. Buddy liked the guitar so much that he had it painted blue and also added the axe's now-famous lightning bolts. Dime saw the guitar in a local store and immediately fell in love with it. He offered to buy it but Buddy wouldn't budge.

Over time, Dime and Buddy became friends, and when Buddy learned the story behind his ML he did something few folks would do, he gave it back to Dime—FOC (free of charge)! "One day Buddy just turned up on my doorstep with a box," Dime remembers. "I opened it up, and inside was the blue Dean. He said, 'Dude, it was your prize to begin with, here ya go!'"

Little Things That Kill

In addition to its custom paint job, Dime's blue ML also featured a locking Floyd Rose tremolo and non-stock pickups. Thanks to his dad, y'see, Dime was hooked on "dicking with shit" and was fascinated with how seemingly small changes, like changing a pickup, could have a major affect on how his guitar both sounded and felt. "My dad hooked me up with a Floyd Rose system and a Seymour Duncan pickup, and they made such a big difference I started paying attention to everything," he admits. "And, before long, I'd found out that I liked Floyd Rose bridges better than Kahlers, this pickup over that one, these frets rather than those—the whole nine yards."

While experimenting with his axe, Dime acquired a Bill Lawrence L500L pickup from a friend and thus began his ongoing love affair with both the L500L and L500XL models. "I think I swapped him a six-pack [of beer, what else!] for it," Darrell laughs. "They're killer pickups, man. The harmonics and clarity are amazing. On the treble strings, it's a real bitch—it sounds like you're running a Cry Baby with the pedal pushed down a bit. It gives you that clear harmonic tone—you get a bit of a pick squeal every time you hit a note up there. And, of course, it's real thick and chunky on the low strings."

Interesting technical tidbit: According to an interview he gave in the April '92 issue of *Guitar World*, whenever he installs a Bill Lawrence humbucker in the bridge position of a gauiter, he "flips" the pickup so the "hot pole is in the front rather than near the bridge."

STOP PRESS: At Winter NAMM 2002, Seymour Duncan launched the SH-15 *Dimebucker* pickup—an aggressive, high-output, hand-built humbucker designed in collaboration with Dimebag himself and bearing his signature.

Since the Dean company was out of business in the late '80s/early '90s, Dime used to scour pawn shops for old MLs and managed to build up quite a collection. Then, a potentially major disaster struck when, after much road abuse, Dime's six-string alter-ego, his perennial "lightning bolt" ML, suffered one headstock fracture too many and had to be retired. As in many good stories though, this seeming misfortune turned out to be a blessing in disguise.

Dimebag Gets an Axe of His Own

After an abortive attempt at collaborating with the newly resurrected Dean guitars (important note: the company who owned the Dean name at the time in question is NOT the same company that's involved now), Dime hooked up with Washburn guitars in the mid '90s. The result was the Dimebag Darrell model, a guitar shaped (wait for it!) almost exactly like a Dean ML. Darrell is the first to acknowledge the similarity: "Hey, if you think about it, even though I didn't design it and don't own the trademark on it, it's my body shape. No one played those guitars besides me!"

A close comparison of a Dime model Washburn and a Dean ML, however, reveals that several subtle alterations have been made to the guitar's shape. The Washburn's back fins are sharper and longer than those on a Dean, and the headstock has been offset slightly and made asymmetrical so as to better complement the body shape. Also, the neck/body joint has been made much less obtrusive than on an ML, making for effortless access to the 22nd fret. As far as Dime is concerned, these subtle shape shifts "make the whole machine a meaner, more wicked weapon."

As expected, the axe comes complete with a Schaller Floyd Rose tremolo system and locking nut, a Bill Lawrence L500 pickup in the bridge and a Seymour Duncan '59 in the neck. "I'm really proud of it," Dime states, er, proudly! "I worked real hard with Washburn to come up with something that speaks to who I truly am. We worked for nearly a year making sure everything was just right—the wood, the body shape and especially the feel of the neck." The Dimebag Darrell model is available in several different guises and Dime-approved finishes, including Dimeslime Green, Dimebolt Graphics and a limited edition Confederate Flag.

Sales of Dime models must be booming, judging from the fact that Washburn has since released two more Dime-designed guitars—the Culprit (a funky-shaped, Explorer-like axe) in the late '90s and the Dime Stealth in 2000. Of the latter, Dime has the following to say: "Basically, it's the regular Dime signature model, but the wings are sharpened and beveled off. It looks like a Stealth Bomber, man, which is how it got its name. The only difference is this: a Stealth Bomber is silent and deadly; this thing is loud and deadly! It's a wicked-lookin' axe—it ain't no candyass shit!"

Amps: Gain, Gain and Even More Gain

"I'd have to say that my tone is mostly the product of the Randall amps I use," Dime professes. "A lot of people think I use tube amps when they hear my tone but I don't, I use solid-state. For what I'm doing I just can't get enough in-yer-face chunk and grind from a tube amp. I won a Randall solid-state half-stack in a guitar contest, and as soon as I plugged it in I knew it was the amp for me. It wasn't perfect right off the bat though. It was a little nasty-sounding and a little fuzzy—kinda like a chainsaw [laughs]. But I liked it and knew that with time I could make it my own sound. And sure enough, it came around."

The Randall amp he won was a 100-watt solid-state RG100H. One of the first things Dime did to "try to clean the sound up a hair" was plug in an MXR six-band equalizer pedal (the blue one). "That little box is killer," he told me way back in '92. "I've tried all the other MXR equalizers, but none of 'em affect my sound in the same way. I've gotta have the blue one." Darrell kept working on fine-tuning his tone and found that combining a Furman PQ4 parametric EQ (swapped for a Furman PQ3 around *The Great Southern Trendkill* era) with his MXR six-band graphic transformed his RG100H and Bill Lawrence-loaded Dean pairing into the instantly recognizable Dime sound we all now know and love. He also employs a rack-mounted MXR flanger/doubler, which is "tucked [mixed] real low but thickens things up" and sometimes acts as yet another gain stage in his signal path. In short, Dime beats the crap out of the front end of his amp in terms of gain. For more specifics on his "gain chain," check out the Q&A section that follows shortly.

Ch, Ch, Ch, Changes

Although Dime used his RG100H to record *Cowboys From Hell*, when it came time to make *Vulgar Display of Power* he reverted to another Randall solid-state head, the 125-watt Century 200 (C200). And he stuck with 'em both in the studio and on the road until Pantera started working on *The Great Southern Trendkill* when he went back to his good ol' carpet-covered RG100H. Why? Was he tired of his C200s? "No, that stuff is cool," Dime told me at the time. "I only dragged my old shit out to do the demos because I couldn't be bothered to break out my full-blown live rig. Anyway, my tone on the demo tapes for the album was ass-rippin', so we figured, 'Hell, it ain't broke so don't **** with it!'"

Once *Trendkill* was recorded though, Dime returned to his C200 heads and has stuck with 'em ever since, until the turn of the new millennium that is! At that point yet another solid-state Randall head surfaced, the Dimebag signature model Warhead.

Dime's Warhead

"The regular Randall heads I've been using kick ass, but I've always wanted a shitload more gain and grit so I've been using stuff on the front end of my rig to get the gain up where I want it," Darrell admits. "My goal with the Warhead was to get it to where it is the most out-of-control amp you can buy. And we did it, man. When you plug in it'll blow your brains out—that's my guarantee! Hell, if I'm putting my name on it, it's gotta kick major ass. It's got a really good, clean channel and the dirty channel has a really cool mid-scoop for the kinda chunk I go for. It also has a nine-band graphic EQ, which gives you unlimited shit you can do with your sound, and 16 preset digital EFX instead of an old reverb knob that nobody uses! The Warhead kicks out 300 watts, too, so it's louder than shit."

Unfortunately, the Warhead wasn't ready in time for Dime to use it on Pantera's 2000 release, *Reinventing the Steel*, so the bulk of that album was recorded with his C200s. This said, a final prototype did make it down to the studio in time for him to use it on a few "face-ripper" overdubs! Dime is understandably proud of his latest signature piece of gear, and it was unleashed on the unsuspecting public in mid-2000.

Hail Me a Cab

Up until the release of the Warhead, Dime was using Randall (412JB) straight 4 x 12 cabinets loaded with 80-watt Jaguar speakers for his dirty sound and Randall (412CB) straight 4 x 12 cabinets loaded with 70-watt Celestion speakers for clean. Now that the Warhead is out though, his whole backline will be changing. "The Warhead is part of a signature stack," Dime explains. "It comes with a 4 x 12 cabinet on top called the Devastator, which is loaded with Celestion Vintage 30s and a 2 x 15 cab on the bottom called the Subsonic Detonator. I've got the 15s happening because when you start chunking out on real low notes, 12-inch speakers start to fart out."

Will having all of this new signature gear result in Dime's signature sound morphing into something completely different and, gulp, less desirable? Hell, it wouldn't be the first time that has happened—compare *Van Halen 1* with *Van Halen 3* if you don't believe me! "My sound is NOT gonna change, bro," Darrell vows earnestly. "Nobody's gonna go: 'Oh ****, Dime's lost it, man!' It's gonna be more like, 'Wow, that's even better.' All I'm doing is honing my tone in."

Bring the Noize...Down!

Another fairly vital component in Dime's rig is a noise gate that he "sets real high to produce the tight, ferocious rhythm punch," which is another of his instantly recognizable sonic signatures. "When we play live, my guitar tech Grady [Champion] is always riding my gate," Dime told me during the band's lengthy *Vulgar Display of Power* tour. "He opens it up for feedback, solos and harmonic squeals and closes it down hard for tight rhythm shit like at the end of "Domination" [*Cowboys From Hell*]. It keeps him real busy, man!" Dime's noise reduction unit of choice? Predominantly a Rocktron guitar silencer.

Interesting aside: When recording *Trendkill,* Dime employed a "beaten-to-shit, cheap little Boss noise gate pedal [NS-2]."

The FX Files

Although he enjoys "dicking around" with FX devices (old and new) and owns a bunch of 'em, Dime keeps his main rig fairly straightforward in terms of stomp boxes. "If you've got time to stand on stage and hop up and down on buttons, you might just as well roll a chair up there and sit on the mother****er!" Darrell roars. "You don't go to war sitting down or standing still, man. I'm up there to rip it up!" Consequently, aside from the gain-adding devices we've already discussed (which are always on!), Dime uses only two devices to further enhance his celebrated tone—a DigiTech Whammy pedal and a wah.

Wah's Up

Over the years Dime has stepped on a Vox wah (V847), a Dunlop Cry Baby, a Dunlop 535Q and a rackmounted Dunlop (DCR-1SR) as well. "Man, that thing is incredible. You can literally get whatever wah sound you want out of it," he raves about the latter. "I also really dig that you can run a bunch of [controller] wah pedals all over the stage with it so you're not always tied to that one spot. The only uncool thing about it is that Rex [Brown, Pantera's bassist] will be dicking me off every night 'cause he'll be jumping on my wah pedals all the time."

In addition to using his wahs in the traditional way (i.e., to create wah-wah sounds!), Dime has been known to use the pedal as a tone filter for certain leads in the recording studio. "I'll just open up the pedal to where I think my sound is hot and then I'll leave it there," he admits. "I don't do that live though."

STOP PRESS: At Winter NAMM 2002, Dunlop unveiled the DB-01 *Dime Cry Baby From Hell*—a Dimebag signature Wah pedal with an eye-catching camouflage finish and unique CFH logo modeled after the *Cowboys From Hell* tattoo the guitarist sports on his shoulder. "It's basically a tricked-out, hot-rodded Wah," Dime explains. "I'm really proud of it, man. It sounds bad-assed and it looks bad-assed too—it's ready for war!"

Whammy King

With his penchant for making high-pitched squeals with his whammy bar, it is hardly surprising that Dime is an expert at producing weird and wonderful noises with a DigiTech Whammy pedal. In fact, he's one of the most celebrated and innovative abusers of this unique unit, using it as an integral part of memorable riffs in songs like "Becoming" [*Far Beyond Driven*] and "Suicide Solution, Part II" [*The Great Southern Trendkill*]. "Philip [Anselmo, vocals] calls it my 'stepping-on-a-cat effect,'" he laughs, "and that's a pretty goddamned accurate description of what it sounds like in 'Becoming.' It really does sound like we were jumping on a cat, with a cord plugged up its ass and some EQ on it!" Actually, when playing live, Darrell has two Whammy pedals in his rig—one on-stage for him and the other off-stage for his tech to use during "Becoming." Why? All will be revealed in **Chapter 10**.

Other FX:

I. Multi-FX

At one time Dime clearly wasn't a huge fan of multi-effects units: "I never understood people who were into those things," he told *Guitar World* back in June '92. "I mean, just what I need—30 different choruses and 75 watery reverbs. I think those boxes were designed for people who either play New Age music or sit in their room, shoot crank [slang for heroin] and go, 'Wow! Far out,' You can spend so much time fooling around with those things that you never get around to practicing."

Time has obviously mellowed his attitude toward such devices, judging by the fact that he appeared in an ad campaign for the Korg G3 multi-effects pedal a few years later. Mind you, the G3 was a simple-to-use pedal rather than one of those ridiculous rack devices that requires a degree in computer science for you to be able to even switch the thing on! He is also a big fan of Korg's pocket-sized Pandora units and even used one on the track "10's" [*The Great Southern Trendkill*] to create a weird fluttering effect that appears briefly. He did so by using the preset "Aqua" on the original Pandora. He also used Korg AX30G multi-effects pedals on both *Trendkill* and *Reinventing the Steel*.

Talking of Korg's ToneWorks products, Dime is also quite partial to their G1, a programmable distortion pedal that is, sadly, no longer made. "The G1 is a bad-sounding little unit," he told me while making *The Great Southern Trendkill*. "I used it on the demos, and some of it made it on the record. If I can't beat a part of the demo, then we'll extract that small section and use it." In fact, as you'll discover in a great story Darrell tells in **Chapter 9**, he even used a G1 to record the brilliant outro solo in "Floods" (*The Great Southern Trendkill*).

II: Stomp Boxes

Multi-effects devices aside, although his stage setup is relatively simple when it comes to pedals, as you're about to discover, Dime is a huge fan of stomp boxes and loves to experiment with them when it comes time to record. "My room is like a pawn shop!" He roars. "I have this box filled with crap, every bullshit effect you could possibly mention." His most adventurous stomp box experiment probably occurred when he recorded the solo of "Fucking Hostile" (*Vulgar Display of Power*). "I couldn't get the lead down, so our producer Terry Date asked me if I had any funky effects. Man, that's the wrong question to ask me!" Dime quite literally grabbed a handful of stomp boxes from his box and chained 'em all together. "I was running two wahs, a cheap-assed Ross flanger, a Mosrite fuzz box, a Boss phaser and an old Boss OD1 overdrive that was caked with brown dirt!" Darrell laughs. "It was a major noise that was totally uncontrollable and I got off on it. After a couple of takes, the flanger stopped working for good, but by that time I'd nailed the sucker. I'd like to see someone try to rip that tone off!"

Other members of Dime's battered 'n' bruised collection of stomp boxes that have made it onto albums include the following: a Boss CE1 Chorus, a Lexicon Vortex, a Roland AP-II Phase 2 plus a "bunch of old Electro-Harmonix shit"—namely a Small Stone phaser, a Little Big Muff fuzz, an Electric Mistress flanger/filter matrix and a Soul Preacher compressor/sustainer.

III. Off-the-Wall Sonic Insanity

As he's already made perfectly clear via both his words and his music, Dime is a huge fan of weird 'n' wonderful noises. Some he creates via inventive stomp box use (especially the Whammy pedal) and others through his trademark whammy bar abuse. On occasions though, he gets into some pretty "off-the-wall shit!" *The Great Southern Trendkill* contains two great examples of Dime's warped creativity. Check out the weird noises that occur during his solo in "Suicide Note, Part 2" for instance. What on earth is going on there? "That's me going off on some completely erratic lead and the noises you're talking about is just me kicking on a Dremel right next to the pickup—it kinda sounds like a power surge!" Darrell explains with a grin.

Cool, but what on earth is a Dremel, Dime? "A Dremel's kinda like a super-high-powered drill, but it's a little-bitty mother****er. It's one of those things you can put all those different bits in the end of it. You can even route a guitar with one."

And what about those really nasty-sounding, distorted chord stabs that jump out of one side of the stereo image during "Living Through Me (Hell's Wrath)"? "That's a Baby Marshall Stack [Lead 12 Micro-Stack] with wax paper taped over the speaker cabinet, being played down a giant cardboard tube with silver foil covering the far end where the mike was," the mad axeman laughs. "And, of course, every control on the Marshall was turned up to 10! I only used that amp for that little effect though; the rest of the album was cut with my Randalls."

Question Time

Right, as promised, we're gonna close this section with Dime answering a couple of questions. They're both interesting, but the first one contains some super-important advice that will always hold true, even though Dime wrote it back in late 1994. So pay heed, amigo!

What's up, Dimebag? I really dig your tone—it's got mega-gonads! How about some advice on getting a ripping sound like yours? Thanx, mate. Walk!

Ian "Binson" Robinson
Northampton, England

"I'm more than happy to let everybody know exactly what I've got going in my rig, but I'm not gonna tell you how I've got it wired up! The order in which you put your shit in line definitely makes a big difference, and that's something you should dick around with for yourself. For example, if you run your wah before all of your forms of gain, it'll sound different than if you place it after a distortion or EQ pedal—it won't be as ferocious or effective. It also makes a big difference if you put certain units in front of your amp instead of in its effects loop and vice versa. For example, my bud Kirk Windstein from Crowbar uses basically the exact same rig as I do, but he wires it up in a completely different way and he's got an awesome sound that's completely different from mine. So, I suggest you take some time and try to wire up your shit in all the ways you can think of until you get the tone you dig the best.

"Another thing I recommend you dick with is using different forms of gain. There are very few amps that can get as distorted as you want 'em to be by themselves, so you've usually gotta heat 'em up a little bit with a pedal of some kind. Anyway, even if your amp has all the gain you need right out of the box, or if you put another form of gain in front of it, then you'll get a completely different type of crunch or distortion. It doesn't have to be a distortion unit either; anything you can get more gain out of is cool—like a graphic EQ or a boost pedal.

"I use a little blue MXR six-band EQ pedal I got from a pawn shop for some of my gain. The cool thing about using a graphic EQ as a form of gain is you can decide what frequencies you want to ass-crunch to by pushing those particular EQ points up more. With a distortion or overdrive box though, the overall tone tends to get distorted. That's why I prefer to use gain units rather than distortion pedals. Altogether I run three types of gain before I even hit the amp—a hot bridge pickup [a Bill Lawrence L500L or L500XL humbucker], my MXR graphic and a Furman PQ-4, which I use for EQ and gain. Because I've got all this gain going on, my Rocktron Guitar Silencer is real important to me—I've gotta have something that'll shut my shit down or there's too much hiss and uncontrollable feedback goin' on when I'm not playing.

"Just so you know, even if you get all the gear I use and wire it up the same way I do, it won't be my sound exactly. Having said that, the rig's there and it's definitely doing something! The bottom line is this: Try to emulate your favorite player's sound only as a basis to help you find your own tone. And don't be afraid to experiment with different amps, pickups, effects, wirings, axes, etc. Try anything and everything—give it all a chance. Most important of all, get your rig rigged the way you want you to sound."

All Padded Up

Hey Dimebag,
I recently saw a picture of you in the studio during the recording of Far Beyond Driven *and I've got a question about it. What is the piece of foam under your strings behind the locking nut for?*
Juey D. Hill
Droitwich, England

"You know how when you pick the strings behind the nut and get that Chinese kinda sound happening like at the very front of Van Halen's 'Runnin' With the Devil' [*Van Halen I*]? Well, when we were cutting 'Slaughtered' in the studio, I wanted the breaks to be real tight and abrupt but I kept getting a weird ringing sound, almost like feedback. I didn't know what was causing the problem. My first stop was the tremolo springs, so I checked to see if the foam was worn out or had shifted position. [Dime puts foam in the back of his axe to keep the springs from making unwanted noises in tight, abrupt stops.—GW Ed.] It hadn't, so my second thought was the headstock 'cos that's the only place where the strings weren't being muted or deadened. I opened up my gate so I could really hear the problem, hit a chord, muted it and, while the ringing was happening, I put my finger over the strings past the nut at the head stick and it stopped. So we put some foam up there, taped it up and that's your picture and the story. Thank you. Next!"

Chapter 5

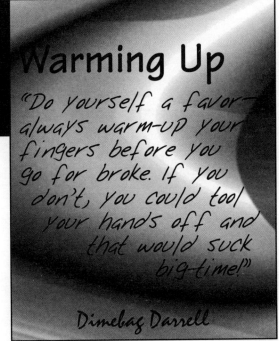

Warming Up

"Do yourself a favor—always warm-up your fingers before you go for broke. If you don't, you could tool your hands off and that would suck big-time!"

Dimebag Darrell

Warming up your hands before you pick up your axe and start blazing is a pretty important habit to form for any player, regardless of experience or style. Think about it, footballers, wrestlers and other professional athletes always warm up before they throw themselves into what they do, and you should discipline yourself to do the same exact thing every time you play. Why? For the same exact reason that all serious sports people do—to prevent injury.

You've only got two hands and they're both vital to you being able to play guitar, so look after them—okay!? If you don't, you could well end up with something nasty like *tendonitis* (a swelling of the tendon sheaths). This affliction is not only darned painful, but it will put your playing on hold for quite awhile because the only cure is complete rest. Please take this warning seriously, amigo: Always warm up or you could end up being a frustrated six-string spectator instead of a participant! Don't take my word for it though; check out what Dime has to say on the subject at the head of this chapter.

Get the picture? Good! Enough of my gab. Here's what Darrell does to warm up his digits every time he plays:

"My warm-up routine is something I've basically been doing since I was real young, and it's where I got a lot of my trilling [combined hammer-ons and pull-offs] chops from. All I do is combine symmetrical trills with chromatics. I start off doing a one-fret trill between the 1st and 2nd frets of the low E string with my index and middle fingers (**Example 2**) and then take the trill across each of the strings in turn from low to high. When I get to the high E string I scoot up a fret and then do the exact same thing back across the strings from high to low. I'll continue to do this all the way up the neck until I get to about the 15th fret. By this time I'll be feeling a pretty good burn in the back of my left hand, so I'll shake it out and get some blood flow happening in my fingers.

Example 2

Guitar tuned to "concert pitch" (A = 440 Hz) (low to high: E A D G B E)

Important Tuning Note

Whenever an example in this book doesn't boast a "guitar tuned to..." note,
the tuning used is "concert pitch" (A = 440 Hz) (low to high: E A D G B E)

"Then I'll do the same exact thing between my index and ring finger (**Example 3**) and then again between my index finger and pinky (**Example 4**). By the time I've done all this, my left hand is real loose."

Example 3

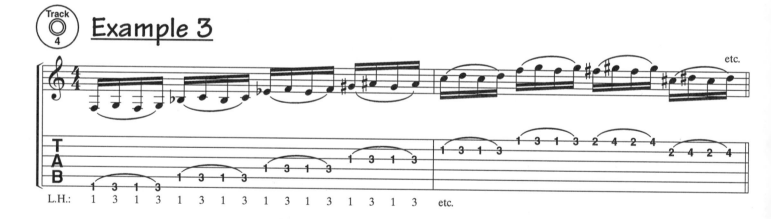

Example 4

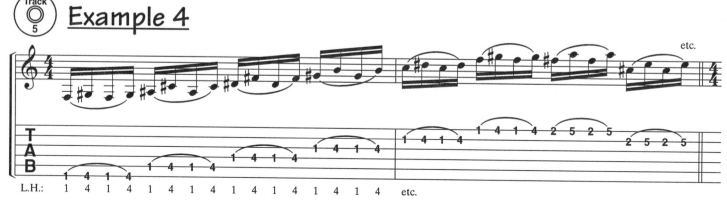

"To get my right hand happening I'll play along with whatever is playing on the dressing room stereo. I don't play the riff or anything though; I just chug out eighth notes [two even notes per beat] on my low-E string using downstokes. If the tempo of whatever I'm chugging along to is too slow, I'll play double-time against it by playing 16th notes [four even notes per beat]. Then, once my right arm hurts from doing that, I'll do some double-picking [alternate picking: i.e., down, up, down, up] shit.

"**Example 5** shows a simple exercise I use that alternates between downstrokes and alternate picking. I'll play this pattern over and over until I feel a burn in my picking arm. Then I'll stop, shake out my right arm, rest for a second and do it over again. Man, after you do this a couple of times, it feels like you've been playing for an hour!"

Example 5

"Once I've done all this, I work on getting my right hand and left hand locked in together by playing some licks and riffs. Then I'm ready to go."

Left for Lead, Right for Rhythm!
"This warm-up routine is great for speed, dexterity and my style of playing," Dime concludes. "When I play lead, y'see, I don't do a lot of right-hand picking. It's more like my left hand is for lead and my right hand is for chuggin' out riffs — it's like left is for lead and right is for rhythm. I believe the technical word for my lead style is *legato* [the Italian word for 'smoothly']. Some guys pick every note when they solo, and that's something I definitely don't do."

IMPORTANT NOTE: When the weather is cold, warming up properly becomes even more important because low temperatures often reduce the blood flow to your hands 'n' fingers. So, make double sure you warm up properly in those winter months, especially if you're jamming in an unheated place!

Chapter 6

First Base: Riffs

A detailed look at Dime's unique form of rhythm 'n' bruise

To me and my band, guitar riffs are what it's all about. We know that every time we jam on a great riff, we've got a fighting chance at a great song. You don't have to go to G.I.T. or know a bunch of weird-assed chords and scales to come up with killer shit; you've just gotta be totally into what you're doing. Check out Judas Priest's *British Steel* album if you don't believe me. It's packed full of god-like riffs from top to bottom, and most of 'em aren't hard to play. If you don't already own this album, buy it—it's essential shit, man! "

Dimebag Darrell

Wow, with a "riffs rule" conviction that strong, it's hardly surprising that Dime's column was called *Riffer Madness*, is it? There follows a bunch of great ideas and insights culled from said column that, according to Darrell, "might help you make the most of a good, heavy riff." As you're about to discover, never has a truer promise been made. Read on, fellow CFH.

Rhythm 'n' Bruise!

"Well-balanced players rip on rhythm as well as leads," states Dime. "As far as I'm concerned, it's no good being able to wail out smokin' leads if your rhythm chops hugg! I've been into playing rhythm from day one, and a lot of that has to do with having a brother who kicks ass on drums. I grew up jamming with Vinnie [Paul, Darrell's brother and Pantera's skin-basher, remember?!] and he definitely taught me the importance of timing and playing tight—and that, along with some great chops, is what rhythm playing is all about."

Metal Muting

"On a lot of our riffs and power grooves I add some serious low-end chunk by applying some heavy-duty palm muting. I always do my muting by lightly resting the outer side of my right-hand [RH] palm [**Diagram 1**] just in front of the bridge. My whammy system is set up so I can yank the bar up as well as do dive-bombs with it [**Diagram 2**]. This means that if I accidentally push down on the bridge with my palm when I'm muting, my strings go sharp and sound outta tune. I make sure this never happens by never resting my hand on the bridge when I'm palm-muting."

Diagram 1

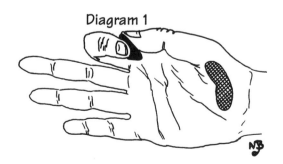

Diagram 2

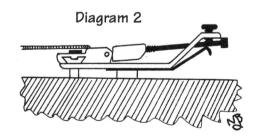

Example 6 is the instantly memorable main motif of "Revolution Is My Name" (*Reinventing the Steel*) and, as you can see, it is heavily spiced with RH palm-muting. To add further beef to this sledgehammer riff, Dime picks the palm-muted, open low E string triplets in the opening bar using downstrokes exclusively.

Example 6: "Revolution Is My Name" main riff

Guitar tuned down one step (low to high: D G C F A D)
All notes sound one step lower than written

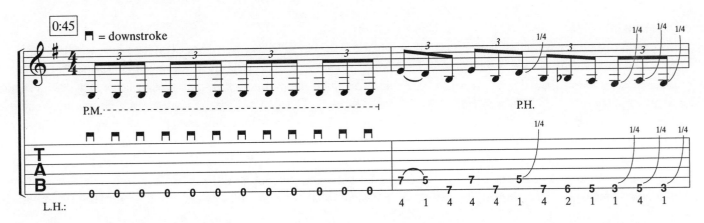

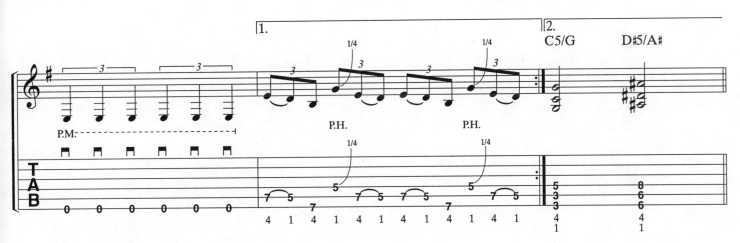

P.H. = pinch harmonic (to be explained shortly!)

The Ups and Downs of Picking

"Whenever possible, I like to play palm-muted chugs like the ones in 'Revolution Is My Name' (**Example 6**) using downstrokes only for maximum heaviness and chunk," Dime points out. "But when the tempo gets past a certain point, alternate picking [i.e., down, up, down, up] is the only way to go—unless you're James Hetfield [Metallica's rhythm ace]! A good example of a Pantera riff that's too fast to pick using just downstrokes is the verse riff of 'Fucking Hostile' (*Vulgar Display of Power*) shown in **Example 7**.

Example 7: "Fucking Hostile" verse riff

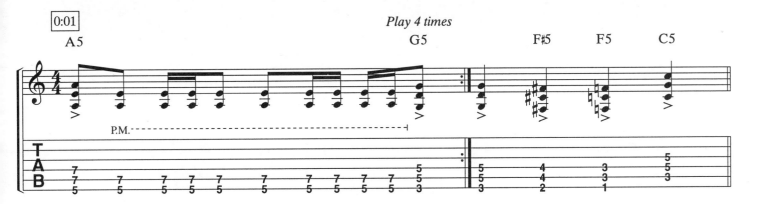

"Even though downstrokes sound heavier, I'm not against up-picking. In fact, I use it a lot. Upstrokes require a different attack than downstrokes and can suit certain riffs better. I often use upstrokes on low-E string notes because I can get a real good scrape happening. I can also dig in deep with my pick and hit the string as hard as I like without having to worry about striking any other strings—think about it!"

Pick Squeals

At this point of the proceedings you're probably thinking, "This is all cool stuff, but what the hell do the two P.H. things in the fourth bar of the "Revolution Is My Name" riff we've just looked at in **Example 6** mean?" So, before we go any further, let's clear that up. P.H. is an abbreviation for pinch harmonic (a.k.a. pick harmonic or artificial harmonic). And what exactly is a P.H? "It's a pick-induced squeal," explains Dime. "I get these squeals happening by picking the note so that the side of my right thumb hits the string at the exact same time as the pick does [see **Diagram 3** and **Diagram 4**]. Exactly where you pinch the string determines what sort of harmonic squeal you'll get happening—if you get one at all! The sweet spots vary from note to note and string to string. So, crank up that gain [distortion definitely helps bring out harmonics] and try using this pinching technique all over the string in the area between the two pickups. Providing you're pinching properly, you'll hear it when you hit that sweet spot—and there is more than one, Dad!"

Diagram 3

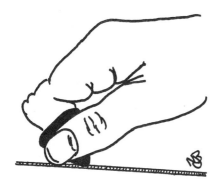

Diagram 4

"This is just one of many trick techniques that you can incorporate into your own style once you nail it. It might take you a while to get it down, but don't sweat it, bro—spend a little time on it, ease up and it'll happen. Then, like I've just said, try applying this squealing technique and every other new technique you learn to anything and everything. Y'know, check shit out!"

Going Down

One of the simplest ways to get some extra low-end grind happening is to use what a lot of guys call dropped-D tuning. It can definitely inspire you to jam out some bad-assed riffs, and it sounds heavier than regular tuning. Just drop your low-E string down to D and leave the rest of your strings where they are. Your axe'll be tuned from low to high: D, A, D, G, B and E. Check it out—hitting the three open low strings gives you a nasty D5 chord [**Diagram 5**]. And you can play any power chord you want using just one left-hand (LH) finger [**Diagram 6**], which means you can slam harder when you're playing live. We use this tuning on the likes of 'Primal Concrete Sledge' [*Cowboys From Hell*], 'No Good (Attack the Radical)' [*Vulgar Display of Power*] and 'A New Level' [*Vulgar Display of Power*]."

Diagram 5
Open D5 shape
in dropped-D tuning

Diagram 6
One finger power chord shape
in dropped-D tuning

◉ = root note

"Also, if you play stuff on a guitar tuned to dropped D just like you'd normally play it on a regular tuned guitar, you might accidentally come up with some cool-sounding riffs. That's kinda how I wrote the "Medicine Man" [*Cowboys From Hell*] riff [**Example 8**]. I was dicking around with a fingering pattern [**Diagram 7**] I knew worked in normal tuning on a guitar with the low E tuned down to D and came up with the riff."

Diagram 7

Example 8: "Medicine Man" riff
Dropped-D tuning (low to high: D A D G B E)

How Low Can You Go?

"Another thing you can do is drop the whole guitar down a whole step (low to high: D, G, C, F, A, D) [as we've already seen in **Example 6**]. The majority of *Reinventing the Steel* was recorded with the guitar tuned like this. Or, if you want, you can even go down a step-and-a-half (low to high: C#, F#, B, E, G#, C#) like I do on a song like 'Drag the Waters' [*The Great Southern Trendkill*]. Tuning that low is nothing new though; Tony Iommi, the total god of the metal riff, was doing it in Black Sabbath way back when.

"Besides sounding real heavy, the cool thing about these two tunings is that your guitar feels totally different—the strings get real loose and spongy. This means you can get some killer wide vibrato happening and do some really big-assed bends like the ones between 3:09 and 3:13 of my 'Walk' [*Vulgar Display of Power*] solo too. I beef up my low E, A and D strings a bit for these tunings [see **Chapter 4**], but they're still relatively loose-feeling 'cos they're tuned so low."

Loony Tunings

Talking of tunings, by this time you may well have already tried to play along with a Pantera recording using a guitar you've tuned with your faithful, tried 'n' tested guitar tuner. If you have, you've probably noticed a slight problem—you're not exactly in tune with the album! Why? I'll let Dime explain: "We're already down something like a quarter of a step to begin with," our subject reveals. "Because of this, when we tune to E we're really just a C-hair sharper than D♯ So, when we tune down a whole-step to D, we're really nearer to C♯ I guess!"

To clarify the situation, I called up Dime's long-serving guitar tech, the highly likable and helpful Grady Champion. "To us, E is really D♯ plus 40 cents on the Korg DTR-1 [digital, rackmount] tuners we use," Grady confirmed. "So, D is really C♯ plus 40 cents, and so on."

IMPORTANT TUNING NOTES

1. As previously stated in **Chapter 5,** whenever an example in this book doesn't boast a "guitar tuned to..." note, the tuning used is "concert pitch" (low to high: E A D G B E).

2. As just pointed out by both Dime and his guitar tech extraordinaire Grady, our subject *typically tunes approximately a quarter tone flat.* This explains why you will sometimes see a transcription claiming a Pantera song is tuned down a half-step (low to high: E♭ A♭ D♭ G♭ B♭ E♭) while Dime says it's in "regular tuning" (low to high: E A D G B E). "Cemetery Gates" is a good example of a case where this has happened. Ditto books and magazines telling you that certain songs (e.g., "Floods") are tuned down one-and-a-half steps (low to high: C♯ F♯ B E G♯ C♯) when, as far as Dime is concerned, they're only one step down (low to high: D G C F A D). Once again, this difference in opinion is due to the unique way Darrell tunes. Please bear this in mind whenever you try to tune your guitar to exactly match a song on a Pantera album.

3. For the sake of convenience, and to (I hope) avoid any unnecessary confusion, each track on the accompanying CD is performed on a guitar tuned as indicated in the example being played rather than the "Pantera way"! So, in this book: E = E, A = A, D = D, C♯ = C♯, etc., as opposed to E = D♯ plus 40 cents, A = G♯ plus 40 cents, etc. Geddit?

Percussive Picking and Power Grooves

"In a way I'm kind of a percussionist when it comes to picking because a lot of my rhythm patterns are almost like drum patterns. Like the riff just before the first verse of 'A New Level' [**Example 9**], which is a hard-driving groove based on one note, the open low-E string [which is tuned down a whole step to D because Dime is using dropped-D tuning for this song]."

Example 9: "A New Level" pre-verse riff
Dropped-D tuning (low to high: D A D G B E)

"I actually came up with the idea for this riff by beating on some chopsticks at Benihana [a national chain of Japanese restaurants]! Most riffs are recognizable by their melody, and the fact that you can immediately identify **Example 9** as being 'A New Level' from just its rhythmic pattern shows you how important timing and rhythm is. In the case of this riff, the focus is on the RH chops rather than the melody. We call riffs like these *power grooves.*

"A lot of Pantera's riffs are tight-assed power grooves like the one we've just looked at. Check out **Example 10,** which is the beginning of 'Psycho Holiday' [*Cowboys From Hell*]. Once again, only one note is being hit (F), but you know exactly what the song is thanks to the rhythmic pattern being pounded out."

Example 10: "Psycho Holiday" intro riff #1

"The verse riff of 'Cowboys From Hell' [*Cowboys From Hell*] [**Example 11**] is another example of a muted open-E string power groove, and this one is syncopated. Before we go any further, I guess I should explain what syncopation is all about, just so we're clear."

Example 11: "Cowboys From Hell" verse riff

Psychotic Syncopation

"All syncopation means is accenting beats that you don't normally accent. If this sounds complicated, don't wig, just hold tight and we'll clean this scene up. Let's say you're chugging out a simple eighth-note pattern on the open low-E string, like in **Example 12**. The notes you'd normally accent would be the ones that fall on counts one, two, three and four. This is shown in **Example 13** [the notes to be accented are indicated by the symbol ">"]. All we have to do to make this basic rhythmic idea syncopated is to accent the notes that fall on the "and" counts instead—the eighth-note upbeats. This is shown in **Example 14**."

Example 12   Example 13   Example 14

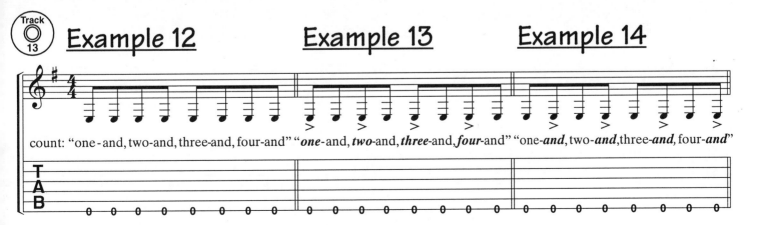

"Now let's apply the same kinda shit to a simple 16th-note groove. **Example 15** is the unsyncopated version (accents on one, two, three and four) while **Example 16** is syncopated (accents *not* on one, two, three and four)."

Example 15

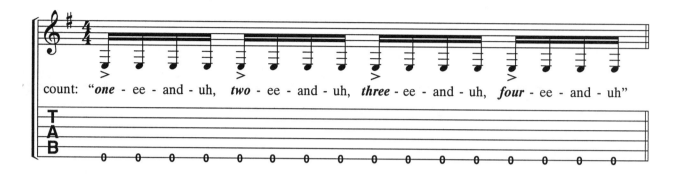

count: *"one* - ee - and - uh, *two* - ee - and - uh, *three* - ee - and - uh, *four* - ee - and - uh"

Example 16

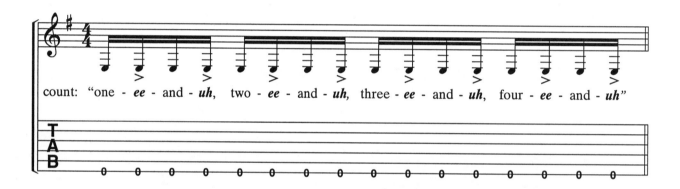

count: "one - *ee* - and - *uh*, two - *ee* - and - *uh*, three - *ee* - and - *uh*, four - *ee* - and - *uh*"

"I know these are real basic illustrations, but remember that simple is bad-assed if done aggressively. So, attack those accents 'cos that's where the magic is! Check out how much more interesting **Example 16** is compared to **Example 15**, which is pretty straight-sounding. And the only difference between 'em is where we've placed the accents. That's the whole trip with syncopation, Pops!

"**Example 17** is another riff taken from the front of 'Psycho Holiday' [*Cowboys From Hell*] that illustrates power grooves and syncopation real well. As you can see, it's made up of a repeated power groove (on the G note at the 3rd fret on the low-E string) and some syncopated power chords that descend chromatically."

Example 17: "Psycho Holiday" intro riff #2

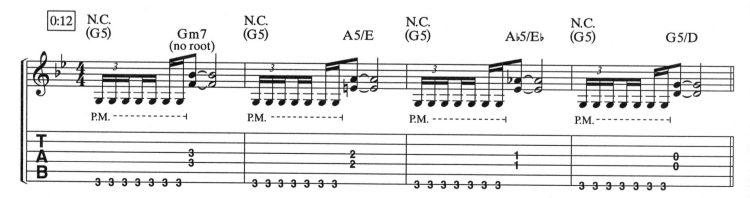

Holes of Silence

"A great way to make a syncopation pattern sound even more brutal is to not play anything in between the accented notes. Doing this can add extra balls to a riff because it makes the accented notes jump out more. For example, compare **Example 18** and **Example 19**. By not playing some of the unaccented notes in **Example 18**, you get **Example 19**—check it out!"

Example 18

Example 19

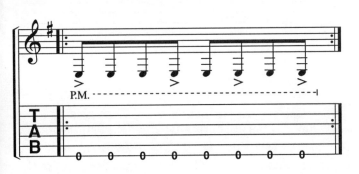

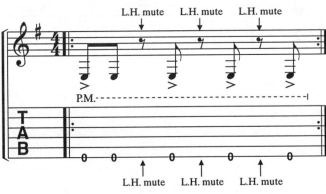

Double-Barreled Muting

"For a riff like **Example 19** to hit home hard, the holes of silence in it have got to be real abrupt. There can be no thunks, clicks, ringing notes or unwanted harmonics goin' on, bro—just silence. To make this happen, you gotta use your left (fretboard) hand to help mute the strings where the rests (holes of silence) occur. Remember, if you're using a heavily distorted sound, you've gotta be quick, clean and precise 'cos high gain doesn't let you get away with any loose shit! There are a couple of different ways of muting with your LH, so let's get to it.

"When I play **Example 19**, I palm-mute the low-E string with my RH all the way through, and I also use my LH fingers to mute it whenever rests occur. I do this by *lightly* laying my left-hand fingers on the string. I've marked these LH mute spots above **Example 19** so you'll know exactly what I mean here. I always use all available LH fingers for muting too. Muting with two or more fingers of your fretboard hand is important because it stops unwanted harmonics from happening. As you'll find out later in this book [see Chapter 8: Third Base: The noise factor], harmonics can occur just about anywhere on any string, especially when you're using a shitload of distortion. So you could easily sound an unwanted one if you use only one LH finger to mute the string—especially if you're not muting with your RH at the same time."

No Place to Hide!

"You've gotta be real quick and precise when you use this type of left-hand muting, BUT don't be too heavy-handed or you'll make unwanted noise by coming down on the strings too hard with your fingers. Using a noise gate will help make the stops and starts abrupt, but you can't use a gate to hide a bad left-hand muting technique—gate or no gate, if you screw up, you'll definitely hear it! You'll know when you get this technique right since it'll be tight and hard-hitting. Keep in mind also that even if you positively crave that tight sound, sometimes a little loose and nasty adds raw coolness! Roll with whatever sounds good to you, man.

"Let's check out another way of muting with your LH by looking at **Example 20**, which is the second interlude in 'This Love' [*Vulgar Display of Power*]. To make this syncopated power-groove crush, you've gotta get the rests between the chord stabs tight and abrupt and, once again, I do this by using both my hands to mute the strings."

Example 20: "This Love" 2nd interlude riff

"If you look closely at **Example 20,** you'll see that I mute the low E and A strings with my RH palm all the way through the riff, so let's zone in on what I do with my LH. It's a real simple technique to get down: As soon as I hit the power chord that comes immediately before each hole, I let my LH fingers come up off the fretboard ever so slightly. I don't actually take my fingers off the strings though—my fingers stay in contact with the strings, they just aren't fretting the notes anymore. This, along with the RH muting that's already going on, mutes the strings completely, killing them dead and stopping any unwanted harmonics from happening.

"With a bit of work, this is something you should be able to do without even thinking about it. To me it's not a trick, it's just a stock part of my playing style. **Example 21** is the chorus riff from 'This Love' and is another good example of this type of two-handed muting in action. Once again, I'm already lightly muting the low E and A strings with my right palm. So, when it comes time to make the holes of silence happen, all I have to do is tighten up my RH muting a hair and relax my LH fingers a tad at the same time. Doing these two things makes the rests tight, clean and silent—all of which are essential for this riff to have maximum brutality."

Example 21: "This Love" chorus riff

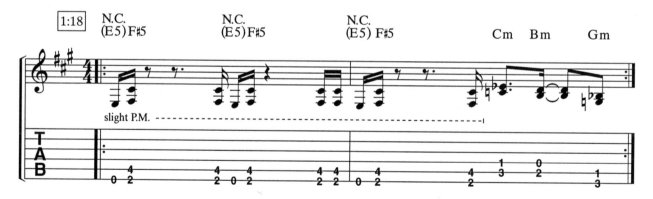

"You can use the same exact approach when you wanna kill fretted chords or notes that you aren't muting with your RH palm—like the riff in **Example 22,** which is from the end of 'Mouth for War' [*Vulgar Display of Power*]. All you have to do here is mute the strings with your RH at the same time you lift your LH fingers off the strings a C-hair. Both muting actions have to happen at exactly the same time for the rests to be clean, so your timing's gotta be right on the money. Oh yeah, one other thing: Don't be too heavy-handed when you bring your right hand down or you'll get some unwanted percussive thunks happening. Dick with this shit and see what you can pull out—it's up to you how tight and abrupt you want your sound to be. Chunk it up and stay hard, Dad!"

Example 22: "Mouth for War" ending riff

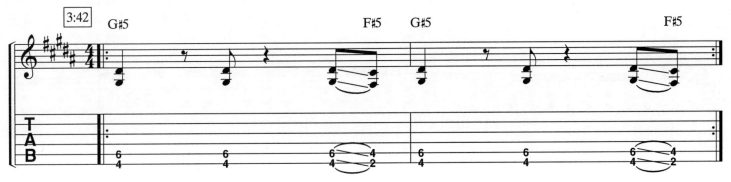

Chromatic Man

"Next up, we're gonna talk about adding some *chromatic* aggression to your riffs."

Game With No Rules

"My musical knowledge is pretty limited, scale-wise. I know the major scale, the minor scale, the pentatonic blues scale and the chromatic scale—that's about it, man! Don't get me wrong, bro, if I can learn a new scale somewhere, I'm definitely open to it. I'm not down on scales, it's just that I'm more into riffing and jamming as opposed to schoolbook theory-reading. Be raw—that's what I always say. I'm always experimenting with new note ideas because in my style there are no rules! Always remember this and never be afraid to cut loose. Hell, if you find yourself hanging on a bad note, you can always tighten it up by bending it, sliding it or yanking on your whammy bar—don't ski on this though, just be open and experiment.

"In case you don't know what *chromatic* means, let me explain: it means every note! So, to play chromatically, all you do is move up and down a string one fret at a time. Simple shit, huh?! I use chromatic thinking a lot in my songwriting. I dig chromatic passages 'cos they can add mood and aggression to a riff. If you've never dicked around with this idea, then check this out. Say you have a riff like **Example 23**:

Example 23

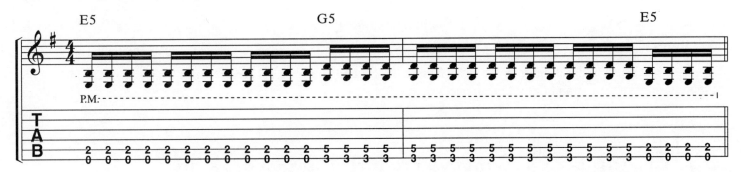

"Instead of just going from E5 to G5 and then back to E5 as shown, try moving between the chords chromatically like in **Example 24**. You can do this between any chords: it just depends what you want to create. This is a simple idea, but it kicks ass. Scope it out and then take it further!"

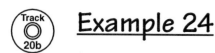

Example 24

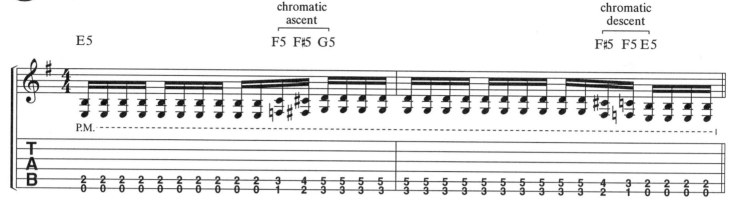

Let the Music Do the Talking

"A good example of a riff that is heavily based on chromatic thinking is the main riff in 'A New Level.' This uses the dropped-D tuning we talked about earlier and is shown in **Example 25**."

Example 25: "A New Level" intro riff

Dropped-D tuning (low to high: D A D G B E)

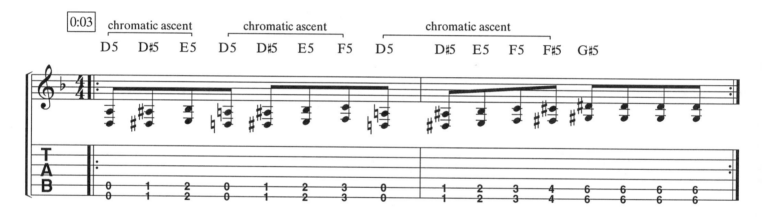

"The pre-chorus of 'Cowboys From Hell' [**Example 26**] and the first bridge riff from 'This Love' [**Example 27**] are a couple more riffs that also involve chromatic shit too."

Example 26: "Cowboys From Hell" pre-chorus riff

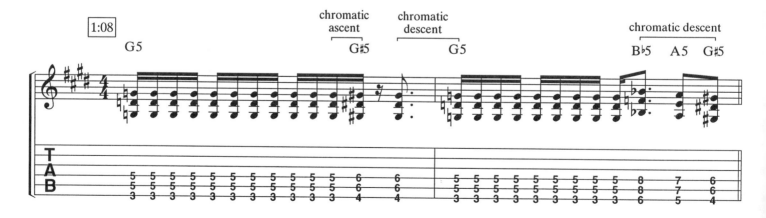

Example 27: "This Love" 1st interlude riff

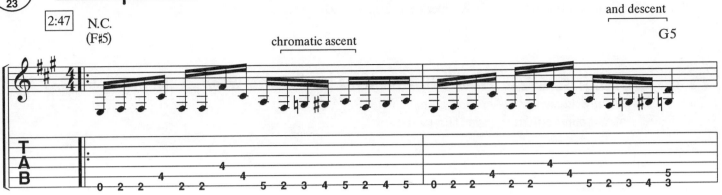

Move It...Chromatically

"Taking a riff and then moving it chromatically up or down the neck can also be a good way of adding tension to a song. I do this sometimes—like in the middle of 'Shedding Skin' [Far Beyond Driven] for example [**Example 28**]."

Example 28: "Shedding Skin" chromatically moved riff

"I hope these few examples will inspire you to jam out some cool chromatic-based riffs on your own. Go for it, keep shredding ass and hang raw!"

Texas Style

"To my ears, using bent notes instead of just playing regular, unbent notes can definitely add a meaner, heavier edge to certain riffs—like the main one in 'Walk' [**Example 29**] for example."

Example 29: "Walk" main riff, the "right way" (with string bends)
Guitar tuned down one step (low to high: D G C F A D)
All notes sound one step lower than written

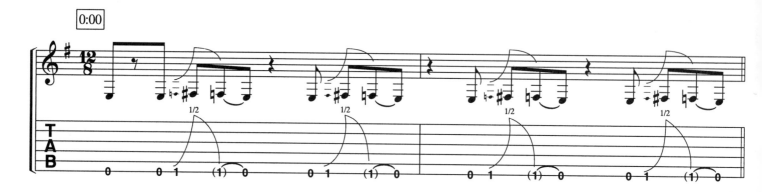

"If I played it without the string bend and release, it'd become **Example 30**."

Example 30: "Walk" main riff, the "wrong way" (without string bends)
Guitar tuned down one step (low to high: D G C F A D)
All notes sound one step lower than written

"I dunno about you, man, but the 'right way' sounds far better to me—it's much heavier and nastier. I call going half-a-note shy of the note I really want to hit and then bending up to it *Texas Style*."

A perfect example of Texas Style in full-blown action is the intro riff to "Revolution Is My Name." "**Example 31** would be the notes in the front riff, but that's not how I play 'em," states Dime. "I do 'em Texas Style like this [**Example 32**]. I also start off with a long-assed slide into the first bend and dig in real hard on pretty much all the bends to get some cool pick squeals going. My style is all about slides, slurs [bends, pull-offs and hammer-ons] and squeals, man!"

Example 31: "Revolution Is My Name" intro riff notes

Guitar tuned down one step (low to high: D G C F A D)

All notes sound one step lower than written

Example 32: "Revolution Is My Name" intro riff, played Texas Style

Guitar tuned down one step (low to high: D G C F A D)

All notes sound one step lower than written

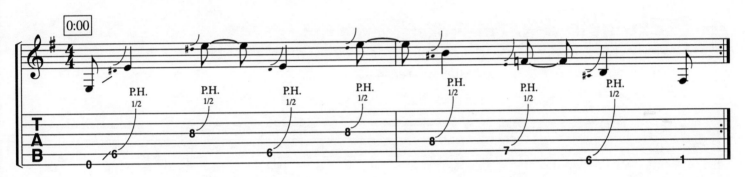

Dissonant Aggressor

Dime often does the same kinda thing with octave diads (a diad is a two-note chord: see **Diagram 8**).

Diagram 8A: Octave diad
on E & D strings

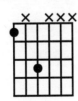

Diagram 8B: Octave diad
on A & G strings

The opening riff to "War Nerve" (*The Great Southern Trendkill*) (**Example 33**) is a good example of this trait in action, as is the verse riff in "I'm Broken" (*Far Beyond Driven*) (**Example 34**).

Example 33: "War Nerve" intro riff
Guitar tuned down one step (low to high: D G C F A D)
All notes sound one step lower than written

Example 34: "I'm Broken" verse riff
Guitar tuned down one step (low to high: D G C F A D)
All notes sound one step lower than written

As you can see, in both of these riffs Darrell bends the octaves up a semitone. Sometimes, though, he just bends each note in the diad up a hair—just like in **Example 35**, the chorus to "Goddamn Electric" (*Reinventing the Steel*).

Example 35: "Goddamn Electric" chorus riff
Guitar tuned down one step (low to high: D G C F A D)
All notes sound one step lower than written

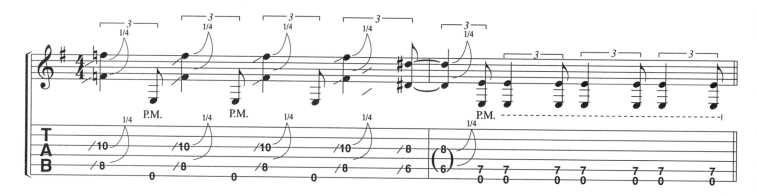

"What I'm doing is sliding octaves on the A and G strings up to F and then bending them sour so the two notes rub against each other," Darrell explains. "It sounds real cool when it's doubled." The best way to ascertain how far to bend each octave pair sour? Sit down with the CD and then, as Dime so subtly puts it, "use your ****in' ears!" **Example 36** is the riff that appears just before the verse of "War Nerve" where our subject does the exact same thing.

Example 36: "War Nerve" pre-verse riff
Guitar tuned down one step (low to high: D G C F A D)
All notes sound one step lower than written

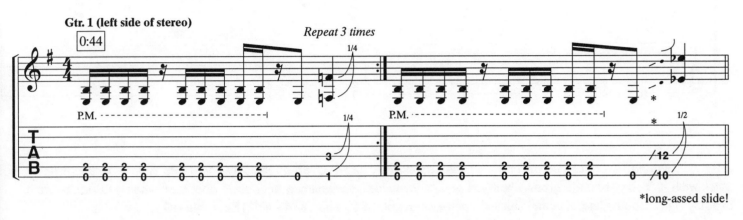

*long-assed slide!

Another good example of the dissonant rubbing Dime is referring to here can be found in the main motif in "10's" (*The Great Southern Trendkill*), which is illustrated in **Example 37**. Playing the bent note in unison with the open G string gives the riff its eerie and unsettling vibe because the two notes tend to rub against each other when they are not exactly identical in pitch, creating a natural chorusing effect. This phenomenon is often referred to as beating.

Example 37: "10's" intro riff
Guitar tuned down one step (low to high: D G C F A D)
All notes sound one step lower than written

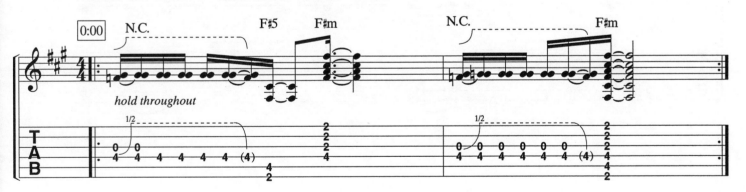

Talking of ways to make a riff sound more evil, back to our teacher.

Power-Chord Bending

"You can do the same kinda deal with power chords too," Dime reveals. "Take a fairly tame riff like **Example 38** for example. To make it more interesting and evil-sounding, try this: Instead of using a regular G5 power chord, hit an F#5 shape and then *bend it up* to G5 like in **Example 39**."

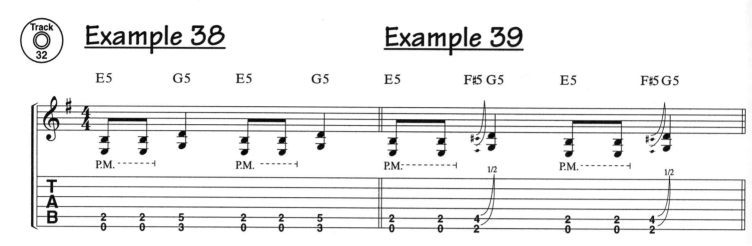

"Bending two notes on different strings up exactly half-a-step at exactly the same time is kinda difficult, but stick with it 'cos it sounds great when you get it down. Hell, sometimes it sounds cool even when you don't nail it exactly right 'cos of the 'rubbing' that happens when you *#%$ the bends up!" (**Example 40**)

Example 40: "We'll Grind That Axe for a Long Time"
"smells like chicken shit" riff

Guitar tuned down one step (low to high: D G C F A D)
All notes sound one step lower than written

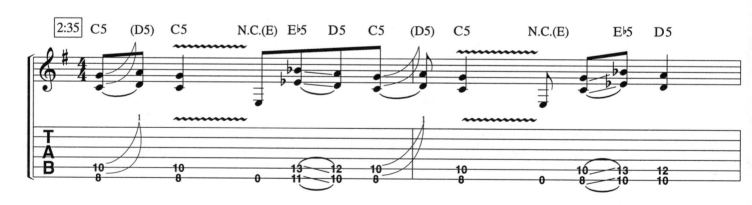

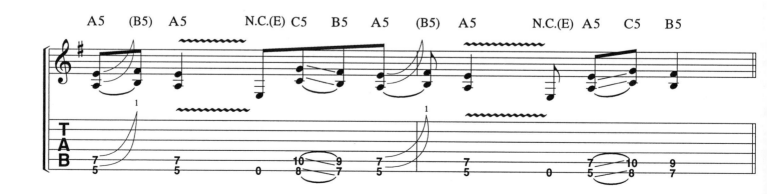

Sinister Slides

"Sliding from one power chord to another can also help a riff sound more sinister," continues Dime. "I got the idea from listening to Tony Iommi in Black Sabbath, and I do it a lot," Dime reveals. The intro riff to "Strength Beyond Strength" (*Far Beyond Driven*) (**Example 41**) and also the chorus riff to "We'll Grind That Axe for a Long Time" (**Example 42**) both feature semitone power-chord slides, which are a definite Darrell trademark. It is worth noting here that when performing the chorus of "We'll Grind That Axe for a Long Time," Dime uses all downstrokes, except in bar 4, where the speed involved necessitates the employment of alternate picking.

Example 41: "Strength Beyond Strength" intro riff

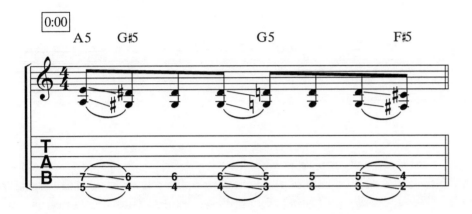

Example 42: "We'll Grind That Axe for a Long Time" chorus riff
Guitar tuned down one step (low to high: D G C F A D)
All notes sound one step lower than written

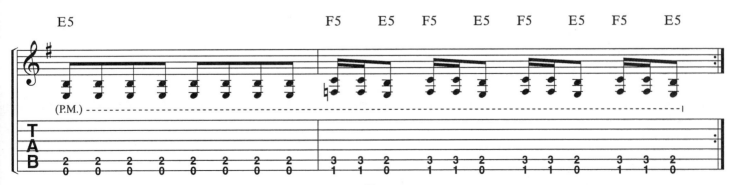

Length Beyond Length

In addition to the short semitone power-chord slides that pepper his work, Dime also likes to use longer slides too—like in **Example 43**, the chorus riff of "Slaughtered" (*Far Beyond Driven*) for example.

Example 43: "Slaughtered" chorus riff

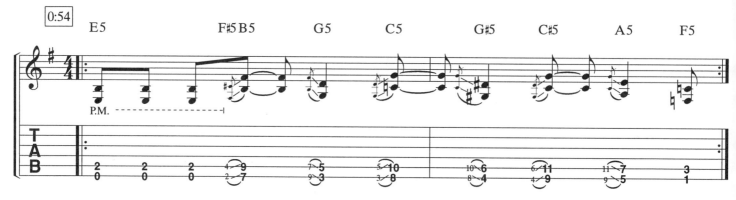

"Sea-sick is what that riff is!" Dime laughs. "Because of the long chord slides it uses, it kinda reminds me of the second intro riff to 'Mouth for War' [*Vulgar Display of Power*] [**Example 44**] except that one is completely smooth and timed out. The 'Slaughtered' riff drags and then catches up—I purposely made the slides up the neck faster than the ones going down 'cos doing that gives the riff the lurching, sea-sick vibe I just mentioned. In fact, the only strict timing the riff has is the muted, low-E string chug that starts it off each time around—listen to the CD to cop the exact way it should be played."

Example 44: "Mouth for War" second intro riff

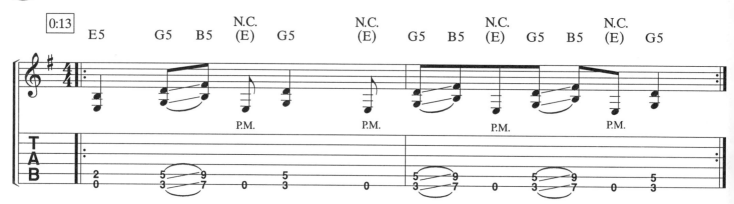

Single-Note Slides

As well as often sliding power chords a goodly distance around the neck, another definite Dime trademark is to do the same exact thing with single notes—and some of the slides he does in this case are extremely long. Like the ones that appear toward the very end of "25 Years" (*Far Beyond Driven*) for instance. "The riff you're talking about is shown in **Example 45** and, like you've pointed out, it does have some long-assed slides in it," Dime confirms. "When you're doing real long slides like these, you've gotta let off the strings a tad with your LH and just let 'em slide under your fingers; if you press down real hard on the strings when you're sliding up or down the neck, it probably won't come out right."

Example 45: "25 Years" outro riff

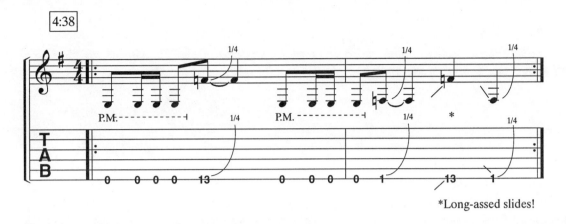

*Long-assed slides!

"Another thing to remember when you're sliding a long way is this: It's the destination that's important. It doesn't really matter how you get there or where you start the slide; the trick is knowing where to stop and making sure that you don't get there too early or too late. So, keep your LH loose, use your ears and eyes and, with a bit of practice, you'll be nailing long-assed slides like those in '25 Years' every time."

Another good example of "long-assed" single-note slides is the verse riff to "Goddamned Electric" (**Example 46**). Providing you follow the guidelines Dime has just given regarding such slides, you should have no trouble mastering this motif.

 Track 39

Example 46: "Goddamn Electric" verse riff

Guitar tuned down one step (low to high: D G C F A D)
All notes sound one step lower than written

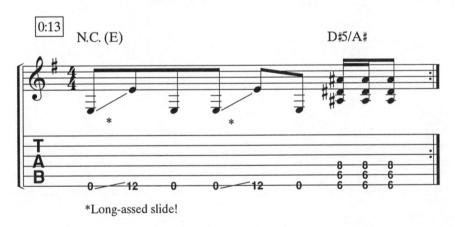

*Long-assed slide!

Striking the Right (Power) Chord

As we've already found, like all metal masters, Dime relies heavily on root/fifth power chords. As we're about to discover, Dime also puts a few other types of power chords to good use in his riffing too, like the ominous A#/D#5 shape used in the "Goddamn Electric" excerpt we just looked at. FYI, it's an inverted power chord.

Inverted Power Chords

What's an inverted power chord? If you're not sure, Dime reveals all in his answer to the below question, which was one of the thousands sent to him while he was writing *Riffer Madness*.

Dear Dimebag,
What the hell is the weird-assed sounding chord you play at the end of the "25 Years" riff that starts with a string scrape? I can't suss it out, bro. Please help me!

Mike Doyle
Los Angeles, CA

"It's just a two-note D5 root/fifth power chord played on the low E and A strings at the 5th fret (**Diagram 9**). Because the fifth (A) is lower than the root (D), it's called an inverted power chord [which is why it is written D5/A]. The reason it sounds kinda weird is that as soon as I hit the chord, I bend it by pulling both strings down toward the floor. To do the pick scrape that starts the riff, I jam the sharp end of my pick between the E and A strings near the bridge and then head for the nut. To make sure there's not a gap between the scrape and the power chord, I just pop the pick upward and out from between the strings at the end of each scrape—by doing this I sound the chord. **Example 47** shows the complete riff. Once again, it's real simple shit, but who cares? It crushes. Just so you know, when I doubled this riff in the studio, I did the pick scrape up on the high strings to fatten up the sound of the scrape."

Diagram 9
D5/A power chord

Example 47: "25 Years" pre-verse riff

0:54

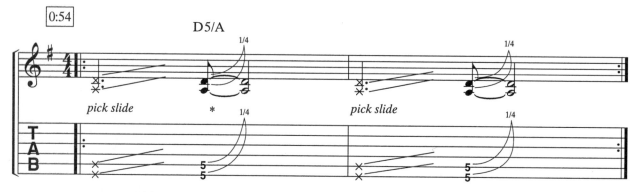

*Listen to CD for exact pitch and timing of bends

Diagram 10 shows a few moveable inverted power-chord shapes for your possible use.

Diagram 10: Moveable inverted power-chord shapes

This done, let's continue with Dime's demonic diad diet.

Schized-Out Power Chords

"**Example 48** is the opening 16 bars of 'Rise' [*Vulgar Display of Power*] and it uses some pretty dark-sounding intervals and chords," Dime states as he pounds out the riff in question.

Example 48: "Rise" intro riff

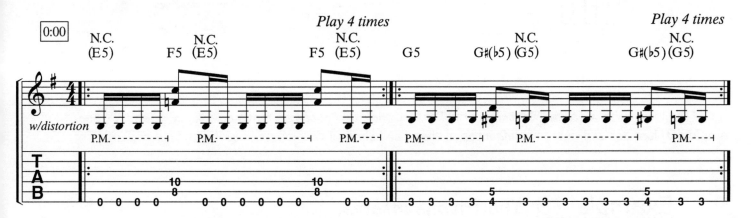

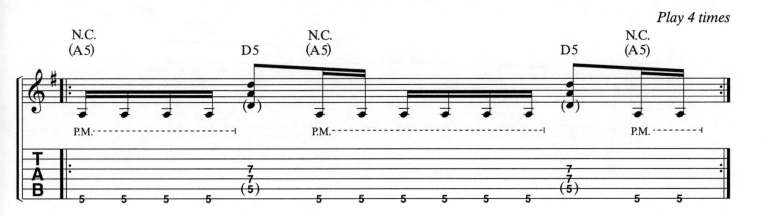

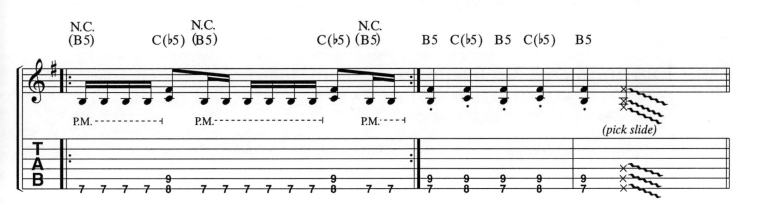

55

"The first interval, E to F [open low-E string to 8th-position F5 power chord] is very powerful, but the riff's frantic tension really builds when we start nailing some diminished-sounding root/flat-fifth power chords as well. **Diagram 11** is a moveable fretboard diagram of one of these chords."

Diagram 11: Moveable root/♭5 power chord

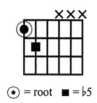

⊙ = root   ■ = ♭5

"The lowered fifth [a.k.a. "flattened fifth," or "Tritone": two notes six frets apart, e.g., E and B♭, see **Example 49**] is a schized-out-sounding interval that can help add tension and heaviness to a riff."

Example 49: The Tritone interval

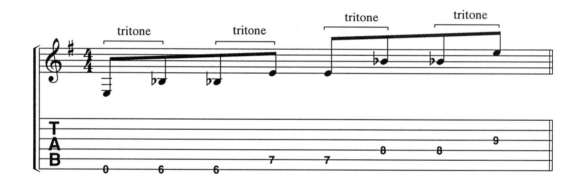

"Check out the main riff to Black Sabbath's 'Symptom of the Universe' [Sabotage] or the opening riff of '13 Steps to Nowhere' (**Example 50**) and you'll hear what I mean. And, as 'Rise' shows, when you play a distorted power chord made up of these two notes (**Diagram 11**), the results can be crushing."

Example 50: "13 Steps to Nowhere" intro riff

Guitar tuned down one step (low to high: D G C F A D)
All notes sound one step lower than written

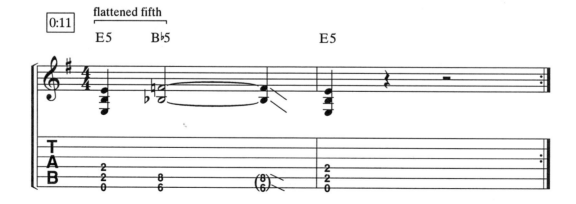

To the Devil His Due

It may interest you to know that the flattened-fifth interval is so demonic-sounding it was named *diabolus in musica*, which is Latin for "the devil in music." And, according to legend, in days gone by, using it was considered a hanging offense! So, it's a good thing that bands like Pantera, Sabbath and Slayer didn't exist a couple of hundred years ago! Anyway, now that the evil-sounding tritone has been explained, let's get back to mastering the diabolical "Rise" intro.

Back Off

"Because the 'Rise' intro (**Example 48**) is so damned fast, I use alternate picking to play it," Dime continues. "Also, to get more cut when performing it live, I roll my treble pickup volume back 10 or 15 percent to eliminate some of the high-end 'fry' and 'mushiness.' When you're using a lot of gain, backing off your pickup volume like this makes your tone a little less overdriven and allows you to better hear the percussiveness of your picking chops. I do this only during the fast picking section of 'Rise' though; once that part's done I crank my pickup volume back up to get the full balls of my tone happening again. Experiment with this idea on your own fast, alternate-picking tunes and see if it helps you out; and don't be afraid to dick with some strange chord shapes too. In fact, don't be afraid to dick with anything—C-scar!"

Major and Minor Diads

"Now that we've scoped-out the diminished-sounding root/flat-fifth chord shape (**Diagram 11**), let's get into some more trick-sounding diads [a diad is a chord made up of two notes, remember?].

"The most common power chord used in metal is the root/fifth, but root/third diads are also worth checking out. There are two kinds of root/third power chords—major and minor—and both sound cool with a ton of gain. **Diagram 12** is a fretboard diagram of moveable root/major-third shape, with the root note on the low-E string, while **Diagram 13** illustrates one with the root note on the A string. **Diagram 14** and **Diagram 15** show the same thing, but with the root/minor-third diad.

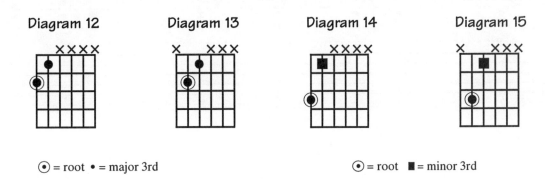

"I've been into these two power chords for a while. One day I was dicking around, playing some single-note shit, and I decided to see what it would sound like if I played harmony with myself by adding a third to each note on the next higher string. That's how I first discovered 'em."

Which One's Best When?

"I don't follow any rules when it comes to using these diads; I just go with the one that sounds best. It's always worth spending that extra second to see if the minor third sounds better than the major third, or just go diminished (**Diagram 11**) and really stretch shit out! For the demonic stuff, the minor shape wins almost every time, but I always run through all of my options before going with it. Sometimes it's cool to play major third and minor third diads back-to-back, or a minor third followed by a root/fifth power chord—whatever combo sounds good. Like I've told you several times before, don't be afraid to experiment and listen! CHECK SHIT OUT!

"To give you an idea of how cool these diads can be, let's get into a couple of riffs that use 'em. **Example 51** is the chorus of 'This Love' we looked at earlier and uses the minor-third shape."

Example 51: "This Love" chorus riff, the "right way"

"Compare it to **Example 52**, which is the exact same riff but played using root/fifth power chords in place of the minor third ones. Once again, man, the 'right way' wins 'cos it sounds a lot darker and menacing."

Example 52: "This Love" chorus riff, the "wrong way"

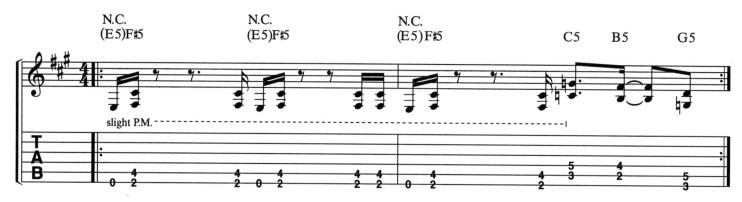

"**Example 53** is a riff from 'Regular People (Conceit)' [*Vulgar Display of Power*] and mixes up regular root/fifth power chords with the major diad shape shown in **Diagram 12**."

Example 53: "Regular People (Conceit)" riff

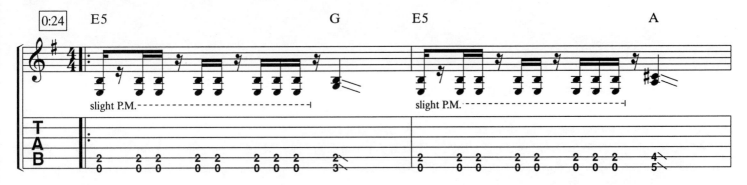

"Check out some of these shapes in your own shit and see what happens. You never know, a major or minor power chord here and there might make a riff more trick'd. So, what the hell, take a wing at it. It's all good, it's a greaz'd wheel!"

The Chord With No Name!

"Remember, it's all good, everything goes and there ain't no damned rules," is one of Dime's many worthy adages when it comes to playing. A good example of his carefree "if it sounds good, go with it" attitude can be found in his answer to the below question that was sent to *Riffer Madness*.

Hey Dime,

*My all-time favorite Pantera cut is "Use My Third Arm." It totally crushes, dude! Anyway, I've managed to figure out how to play all of it except for one single ****in' chord, and it's driving me far beyond insane! What's the shape you use during the intro and verse, bro? I've tried everything I can think of and nothing sounds right. Please help me before they lock me in a padded cell and throw away the key!*

Ed Proctor
Fort Worth, TX

"That's a real ****ed-up chord and, to be honest with you, I'm not even sure what it's called! My guitar is detuned a whole tone (low to high: D, G, C, F, A, D) for that song, so everything sounds a whole-step lower. The chord shape you're talking about is shown in **Diagram 16**. I guess it's an inverted E♭ power chord with an F, the second, added onto the low-E string—if there is such a chord! Remember—like I've said more than once in this column—there are no rules. If something sounds good, run with it, bro! Just so you know, we use this particular chord shape quite a bit on *Far Beyond Driven*—like in the middle sections of 'Slaughtered' and 'Shedding Skin.'"

Diagram 16: the "chord with no name!" (E♭5/B♭add2)

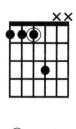

⊙ = root

By Demons Be Driven (Again!): Evil Intervals

As Dime pointed out a short while ago when discussing the "Rise" intro, the flattened fifth is a pretty "schized-out interval." As already mentioned, the flattened fifth was even dubbed *diabolus in musica* because of its inherently evil vibe. Not surprisingly, this interval is used a lot by Pantera, as are the two other most disturbing-sounding intervals known to man—the *minor second* (two notes a half-step apart, E to F for example) and the *major seventh* (an octave minus a half-step, for example, E to D♯).

The "Jaws Theme"-like intro to "Drag the Waters" (*The Great Southern Trendkill*) (**Example 54**) is a great example of Dime using the minor second interval to great effect, and so is **Example 55**, the interlude riff that appears between the second and third verses of "Strength Beyond Strength."

Example 54: "Drag the Waters" intro riff

Guitar tuned down one-and-a-half steps (low to high: C♯ F♯ B E G♯ C♯)
All notes sound one-and-a-half steps lower than written

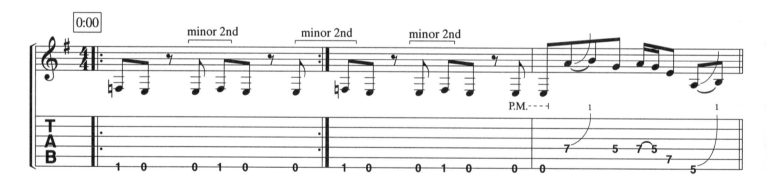

Example 55: "Strength Beyond Strength" interlude riff

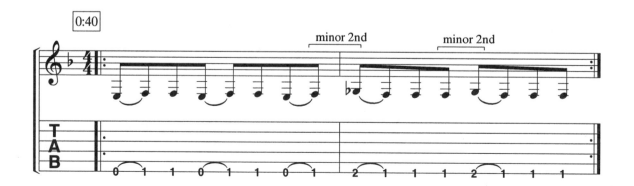

Evil Twins

Example 56 is the pre-chorus of "Goddamn Electric." "It's just the open low-E string with three notes on the A string," Darrell observes. "There's a cool tension on either side of the E though." The tension he is referring to occurs in the second bar where he:

1. Combines the open low-E note with the F note at the eighth fret on the A string (a minor second interval plus an octave)

And then:

2. Combines it with the D# note at the sixth fret (a major seventh interval).

Example 56: "Goddamn Electric" pre-chorus riff

Guitar tuned down one step (low to high: D G C F A D)
All notes sound one step lower than written

Dime doesn't only call on "schized-out" intervals when riffing it up with maximum distortion. As **Example 57** illustrates, he uses the tritone for maximum unsettling effect in one of the bands more mellow moments, the verse riff of "This Love."

Example 57: "This Love" verse riff

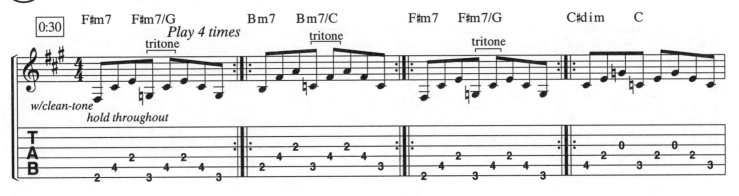

Mr. Clean

Talking of playing it clean, the haunting intro motifs to both "Cemetary" (*Cowboys From Hell*) (**Example 58**) and "Floods" (*The Great Southern Trendkill*) (**Example 59**) are distortion-free Dime moments that are definitely worthy of note.

Example 58: "Cemetary Gates" intro riff

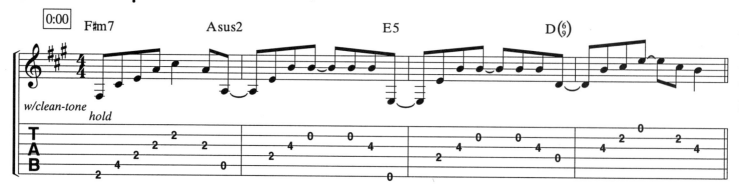

Example 59: "Floods" intro riff

Guitar tuned down one step (low to high: D G B F A D)
All notes sound one step lower than written

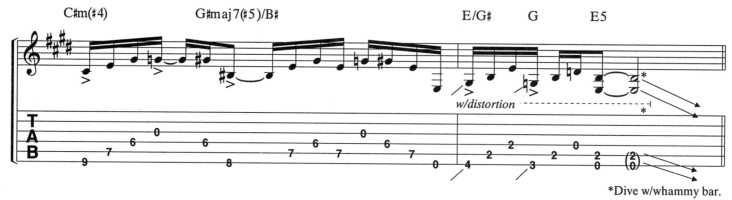

*Dive w/whammy bar.

Both of the above excerpts call on some fairly unusual chord shapes and also require a good deal of RH picking accuracy due to the string-hopping involved. The wide LH stretch required to finger the C♯m (add♯4) chord (**Diagram 17**) in "Floods" could also prove to be quite a challenge.

Diagram 17: C♯m (add♯4)

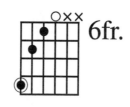

6fr.

● = root

Of all of Dime's mellower moments though, my own personal favorite is the repeated one-bar riff he solos over in "10's," which is shown in **Example 60**. In addition to being a gloriously memorable motif and a great pattern to solo over, this syncopated riff will certainly push your ability to accurately string-hop with your pick to the limit!

Example 60: "10's" under-the-solo riff

Guitar tuned down one step (low to high: D G C F A D)
All notes sound one step lower than written

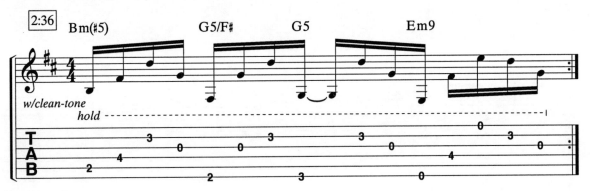

Pedal to the Metal

As you may have noticed, the last three riffs we just looked at all made good use of open strings. Talking of open strings, an incredibly common heavy metal trait is use of the open low-E string notes as pedal tones. Just in case you aren't aware, a pedal tone (a.k.a. *pedal point*) is a note that's frequently repeated (pedaled!) during the course of a riff. The reasons this is done? A frequently repeated low note not only adds weight to a part, but it also helps drive a riff along—especially if the pedal point note is palm-muted. For example, the open low E string note is used as a palm-muted pedal point in the intro riffs to both "Domination" (*Cowboys From Hell*) (**Example 61**) and "Yesterday Don't Mean Shit" (*Reinventing the Steel*) (**Example 62**).

Example 61: "Domination" intro riff

Example 62: "Yesterday Don't Mean Shit" intro riff

Guitar tuned down one step (low to high: D G C F A D)
All notes sound one step lower than written

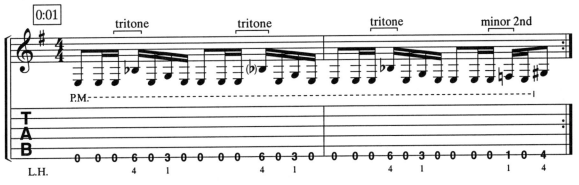

Even more interesting is the second intro riff to "Where You Come From" (*Official Live: 101 Proof*) (**Example 63**), which uses no fewer than three open string notes as pedal points! As marked above **Example 63**, first up is the open D string pedal point followed by the open A and then the open E.

Example 63: "Where You Come From" 2nd intro riff

Guitar tuned down one step (low to high: D G C F A D)
All notes sound one step lower than written

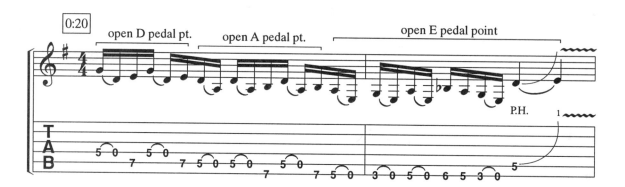

Odd Time Signatures

Although most of Pantera's riffs revolve around a straight 4/4 time signature, every now and again something off-kilter creeps in—like the 7/16 verse riff of "I'm Broken" (**Example 34**) we looked at earlier, which also features some trademark half-step octave bends. Another good example of this relatively unusual Pantera trait is "We'll Grind That Axe for a Long Time," which boasts some 7/4 sections. **Example 64** is the opening salvo and **Example 65** is the main verse riff.

Example 64: "We'll Grind That Axe for a Long Time" intro riff

Guitar tuned down one step (low to high: D G C F A D)
All notes sound one step lower than written

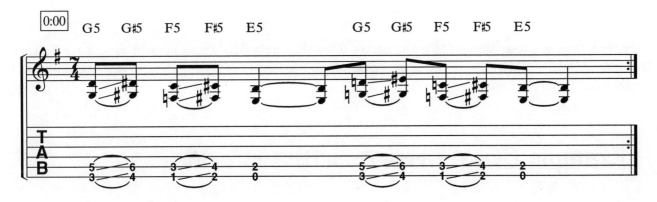

Example 65: "We'll Grind That Axe for a Long Time" verse riff

Guitar tuned down one step (low to high: D G C F A D)
All notes sound one step lower than written

As is the case with the "I'm Broken" verse riff, despite the seemingly complex and confusing nature of the time signature involved, the two 7/4 "We'll Grind That Axe for a Long Time" excerpts are so instantly memorable (read: "singable") you should have no problem nailing 'em after merely a few listens. If you want to challenge yourself by trying to suss them out without listening to the CD first though, tap your foot and count "one, two, three, four, five, six, sev, one, two, three," and so on. Shortening "seven" to "sev" will help you keep constant time.

Octave Repeats

"One of our audience's favorite riffs is the main one from our encore, 'Cowboys From Hell' [Cowboys From Hell]," Dime reveals. "It's a pretty easy riff to play 'cos it's made of the first rock scale we all learn—the E minor blues scale (**Diagrams 18A & 18B**)."

Diagram 18A: E minor blues scale
in open position

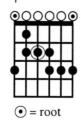

⊙ = root

Diagram 18B: E minor blues scale
in 12th position

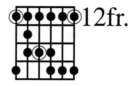

"The first time you hear this riff is in the song's intro (**Example 66**), where I play it an octave higher than I do during the rest of the track. Hearing it played an octave higher is kinda like an appetizer—it introduces you to the riff and makes you hungry for more!"

Example 66: "Cowboys From Hell" intro riff

(Track 57)

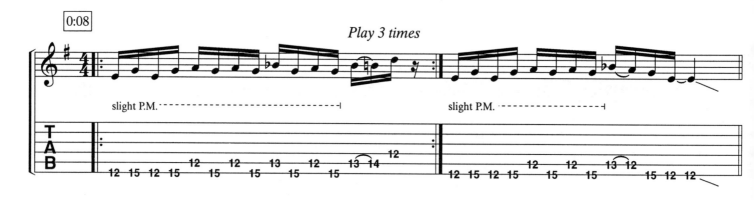

"Playing it higher first also makes the full-blown version (**Example 67**) sound real heavy when it kicks in. I guess you could say that **Example 66** is the body blow and **Example 67** is the knock-out punch. To give the main 'Cowboys' riff even more balls, I play power chords on the E and A notes instead of just playing single notes like I do in the intro version."

Example 67: "Cowboys From Hell" main riff

(Track 58)

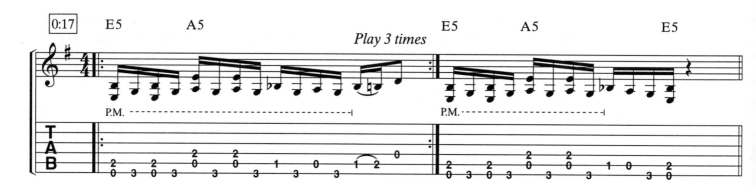

"I also use the idea of repeating a riff in different octaves during the middle 8 of 'Cowboys' (**Example 68**) too. There's a short, one-bar descending run halfway through the bridge (bar 4), which I play again at the end (bar 8), but that time I do it an octave higher. This definitely makes the bridge sound cooler than if I just played the run in the same place twice."

Example 68: "Cowboys From Hell" middle-8 riff

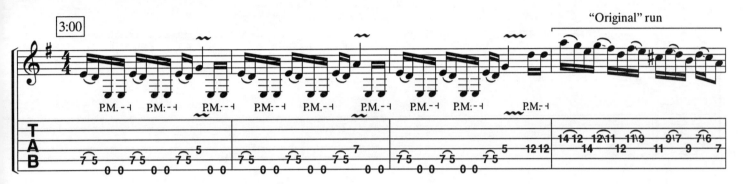

Another good example of Dime repeating part of a riff in different octaves appears in the pre-verse riff from "13 Steps to Nowhere" shown in **Example 69**.

Example 69: "13 Steps to Nowhere" pre-verse riff

Track 60

Guitar tuned down one step (low to high: D G C F A D)
All notes sound one step lower than written

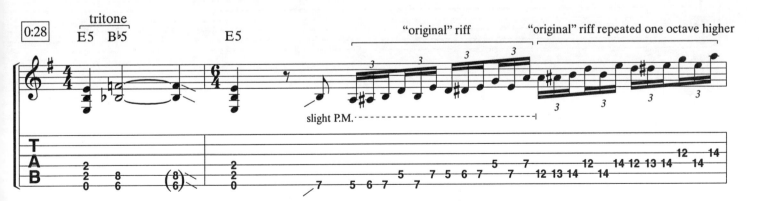

Going for Girth

If you've ever seen a transcription of "Cowboys From Hell," the chances are good that the intro riff (**Example 66**) was shown being played in the wrong position of the neck, namely the 7th instead of the 12th. The "wrong way" in question is shown in **Example 70**.

Example 70: "Cowboys From Hell" intro riff, the "wrong way"

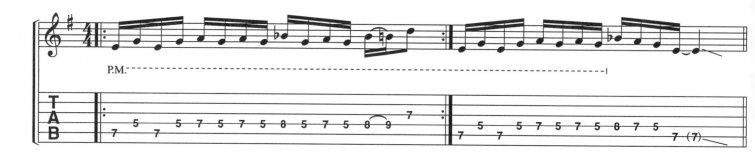

If you compare the two versions of this riff, the notes may be identical but they do sound a tad different. The "right way" is slightly darker and thicker sounding. This is no accident; Dime chose the 12th position version for that exact reason—thicker strings offer extra girth. And he's not alone in this line of thought either. The main riff of Black Sabbath's "Paranoid" (*Paranoid*), one of the most famous metal riffs ever written, is also performed in the 12th position for the exact same reason—Tony Iommi preferred the darker sound it offered over playing the riff in the 7th position. Ironically enough, "Paranoid" is often wrongly transcribed as being played in the 7th position too!

The southern-flavored breakdown riff that occurs immediately after the first chorus of "Revolution Is My Name" is another good example of Dime going for girth and is shown in **Example 71**.

Example 71: "Revolution Is My Name" breakdown riff, played the "right way"

Guitar tuned down one step (low to high: D G C F A D)
All notes sound one step lower than written

68

"When the riff goes up at the end, I don't go to the G string like some people might; instead I stay on the D string because I want the extra girth of that string," Darrell states, playing it the "wrong way" (**Example 72**) to illustrate his point. "You can play it either way, of course."

Example 72: "Revolution Is My Name" breakdown riff, played the "wrong way"

Guitar tuned down one step (low to high: D G C F A D)
All notes sound one step lower than written

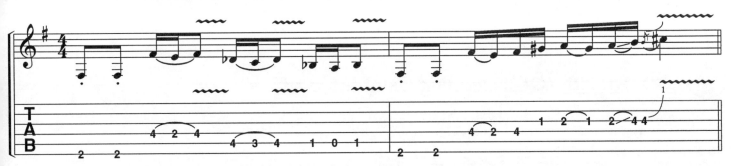

A further example of going for girth is the second intro riff in "Drag the Waters." **Example 73** shows it being performed the "wrong way" while **Example 74** shows the Dime-approved method. As is the case with the other two riffs, when you compare the "wrong" and "right" versions, the difference is subtle but definitely noticeable to a discerning ear with a leaning toward the darker side of tone!

Example 73: "Drag the Waters" intro riff #2, played the "right way"

Track 62

Guitar tuned down one-and-one-half steps (low to high: C♯ F♯ B E G♯ C♯)
All notes sound one-and-one-half steps lower than written

Example 74: "Drag the Waters" intro riff #2, played the "wrong way"

Guitar tuned down one-and-a-half steps (low to high: C♯ F♯ B E G♯ C♯)
All notes sound one-and-a-half steps lower than written

To close this highly informative chapter, we're going to leave you with a few riff-related questions and answers from Dime's aptly named "Feedback Sack" section of *Riffer Madness*.

Shedding Skin, Part 1: The Intro

How the hell do you play the intro riff in "Shedding Skin" [Far Beyond Driven]? That song kicks ass and your column rules!

Brendan "Rob Halford rules" Kelly
Long Island, NY

"This is about the twenty-fifth 'Feedback Sack' letter I've had requesting this riff, so I guess I should get it out there. **Example 75** is your answer, Brendan."

Example 75: "Shedding Skin" intro riff

Shedding Skin, Part 2: The Verse

*My favorite Pantera cut ever is "Shedding Skin." I've nailed the intro/chorus riff but I can't work out what the *#@* chords you're playing in the verse and neither can my friends. They sound like real complicated, hard-to-finger jazz shapes. Help us out dude—please!*

Ben Norton
Spokane, WA

"Usually the hardest-sounding riffs are simple. But because the human mind automatically thinks that hard-sounding shit must be tough to play, you usually get lost killing yourself trying to suss out a part when there may not have been much to it anyway. This riff is a perfect example of this. All I'm doing in the verse of 'Shedding Skin' (**Example 76**) for the most part is just holding down one chord shape (**Diagram 19**) and moving it up a fret (**Diagram 20**) and down a fret (**Diagram 21**) from its natural starting position. You know: dick with shit, and if it sounds cool go with it. That's all I did here. It's simple, but this doesn't make me think any less or more of a riff if my ears like it and it moves me!"

Example 76: "Shedding Skin" verse riff

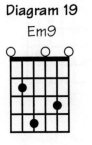

Diagram 19
Em9

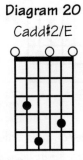

Diagram 20
Cadd#2/E

Diagram 21
Bbm6#11

Shedding Skin, Part 3: The Pre-Chorus

Hey Dimebag,
Your column is king, man! I've learned a bunch from it, especially from the Q&A shit you've been doing lately. Here's my question: What are those weird-assed chords you play right before the chorus of "Shedding Skin"? They're wicked-sounding but I can't find 'em. Please help me out here, bro. Lata!

Hugh Gilmartin
Huntington, NY

"Right off the bat you're gonna need another guitarist or tape machine to help you cop this section 'cos there are two guitar parts on the record. The original distorted guitar part plays **Example 77**, but it just sounded too fashionable, so I ****ed around until I found something that sounded real bizarre and laid that on top of it."

Example 77: "Shedding Skin" original pre-chorus riff

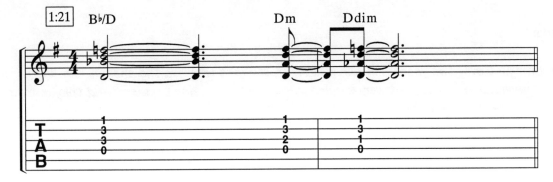

"I didn't even want to use the chord shapes I would normally make and, after dicking around for a while, I came up with three weird chord shapes (see **Diagrams 22–24**) that worked real well over the original three chords (see **Diagrams 25–27**)."

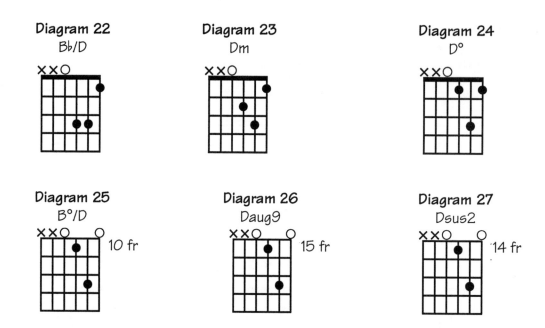

Diagram 22
Bb/D

Diagram 23
Dm

Diagram 24
D°

Diagram 25
B°/D
10 fr

Diagram 26
Daug9
15 fr

Diagram 27
Dsus2
14 fr

"The overdub part I played is shown in **Example 78,** and this is the one you hear the most on the record. It was done with a clean tone, and I used my whammy bar as indicated to mess up the sound of those three ****ed chords some more too."

Track
65

Example 78: "Shedding Skin" overdub pre-chorus riff

Right Speaker

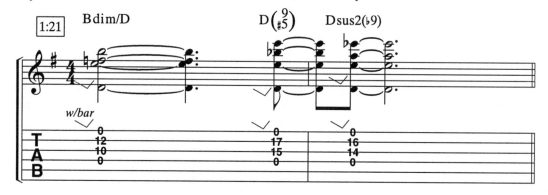

Slow but Sure

Dear Dime,
I've been playing for just over two years and can wail on pretty fast riffs like the ones in "Cowboys From Hell." But I have real trouble nailing some of your slower, simpler-to-play grooves. I don't understand this, man! Slow riffs should surely be easier to play than fast ones.

Ryan Rhodes
Sydney, Australia

"That's a good question, bro. Some people think that playing fast takes a whole lot of time, but I'll tell ya, playing real slow and being able to keep in the groove without rushing the beat is the shit too! For example, my buds in Crowbar jam on some real slow, heavy riffs and they definitely ain't as easy to play as they may seem. You gotta pay real close attention to the groove of the song and you've also gotta resist the temptation to rush. Hang loose, hold back and let your ears, not your fingers, decide when you should hit the next note!"

Hard Chord, Sunken Cheeks

What's the real evil-sounding chord you use over and over during the fadeout outro of "Hard Lines, Sunken Cheeks" [5:42 - 6:56]? It stomps my ass in a major way and I just can't suss it out. I've been playing a regular C5 power chord at the 3rd fret [Diagram 28], but it just doesn't sound heavy enough.

Will Halliday
Hawaii

Diagram 28: *C5 power chord*

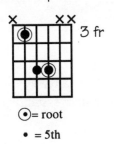

⊙= root
• = 5th

"Remember the inverted power chord shape I told you about when I answered a question about the verse of '25 Years' [chord shape shown again in **Diagram 29** below]? Well, the chord shape I use at the end of "Hard Lines, Sunken Cheeks" [*Far Beyond Driven*] is just a bigger version of that. All I'm doing is taking the C5 shape you're talking about and adding the G note [the fifth of the chord] at the 3rd fret of the low E string like in **Diagram 30**. Doing this doubles up the G note at the 5th fret of the D string and makes the chord real heavy-sounding. You could also throw in the C notes at the 5th fret on the G string too [**Diagram 31**] if you wanted the chord to sound even bigger. The whole riff is shown in **Example 79**."

Diagram 29:
Moveable inverted
Power-chord shape

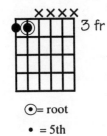

Diagram 30:
C5/G Version 1

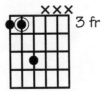

Diagram 31:
C5/G Version 2

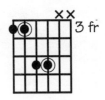

⊙= root
• = 5th

Example 79: "Hard Lines, Sunken Cheeks" outro riff

Guitar tuned down one step (low to high: D G C F A D)
All notes sound one step lower than written
"Because this C5/G chord is real close to the nut, when you slide off it it's difficult to make the slide sound

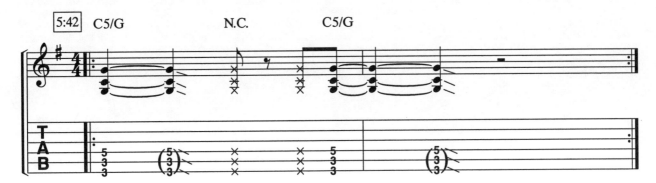

long 'cos you don't have much room to play with. So when my index finger reaches the nut I don't stop the slide, I just lift that finger off the strings so it jumps over the nut, and I keep the slide going with my little finger. Doing this makes the slide sound longer. Practice this sliding idea slowly at first so you don't **** up your index finder by smashing it into the nut! As you get more confident, build up speed. Once again, it's real simple shit that works, man!"

What Key?

Thanks to Riffer Madness, I wrote some really cool riffs with dropped-D tuning, using chromatics. How do I determine the key each one is in?

Ammon "Ambag" Torrenson
Chicago, IL

"That's a tough one to answer without actually hearing the riffs. So I'd say check out the note or chord you play most in a riff 'cos that's probably the root. And if you still can't tell, don't worry; it don't really matter anyway—anything goes. Anyway, I gotta unhook. I hope these answers might crank you open one more notch and help expand your playing forever, stronger than all."

Chapter 7

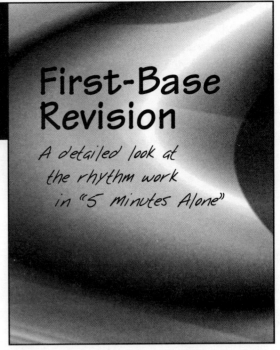

First-Base Revision

A detailed look at the rhythm work in "5 Minutes Alone"

In this section, Dime takes us on a *Riffer Madness* recap jam by taking us on a riff-by-riff guided tour of a Pantera classic.

"What's up? We've just rapped about a shitload of playing ideas that can spice up your rhythm chops, which are all good and are all important. Now I reckon we should take a quick look back at some of the things we've covered, so let's regroup and tighten shit up. We're gonna do this by applying some of these ideas and techniques in a straight-driving tune called '5 Minutes Alone' from our *Far Beyond Driven* album. Enough talk—let's jam."

D-Tune

"In this song my whole guitar is tuned down a whole-step, so the strings go [from low to high] D, G, C, F, A, D. Like I said way back at the start of **Chapter 6**, along with sounding heavy, one of the cool things about this tuning is that your guitar feels totally different—the strings are loose and spongy, which enables you to do some real stretchy shit."

Raw Power

"The opening/chorus riff (**Example 80**) of this cut uses power-chord slides and also has you working on your *muting technique* to make the riff come across right."

Example 80: "5 Minutes Alone" intro/chorus riff

Guitar tuned down one step (low to high: D G C F A D)
All notes sound one step lower than written

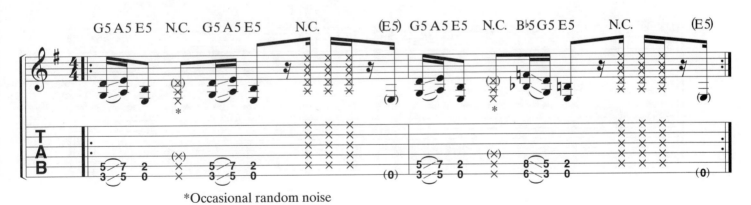

*Occasional random noise

"I wanted this one to sound just like the original demo—loose [noise] gate, nasty around the edges, raw and live-sounding. Ain't nothing wrong with some noise! The ka-chu-ka sound at the end of each bar is a loose left-hand mute around the 3rd fret, and the picking action I use is up, down, up. Make sure you mute the strings with more than one finger to prevent unwanted harmonics."

The Meandering Run

"Next up, let's take a look at **Example 81,** the slippery-sounding single-note meandering run that happens before each verse. This run uses three techniques we covered in **Chapter 6**—string slides, chromatic runs and the tritone interval (G to C♯ and vice versa). After compounding these three techniques, the riff begins to get pretty ****in' heavy!"

Example 81: "5 Minutes Alone" meandering pre-verse run

Guitar tuned down one step (low to high: D G C F A D)
All notes sound one step lower than written

A Double Dose of Evil

"The verse riff (**Example 82**) starts with a palm-muted syncopated power groove that uses an open E5 chord (**Diagram 32**). Pay close attention to the picking action indicated below the tablature. Then, at bar 3, I scoot my fretting finger back a fret to create a real dark-sounding chord [the E♭5/E shown in **Diagram 33**]. This chord is kinda like the root/flat-fifth diad we talked about in **Chapter 6** but with an extra-high note thrown in too. [The "extra-high note" Darrell is referring to here is the D♯ at the 1st fret on the D string, the major seventh of E. This means this shape features two "evil intervals"—the tritone and the major seventh]. I add to the tension of this chord by not muting the strings at all, switching to playing all downstrokes and putting some muscle to it!

Example 82: "5 Minutes Alone" verse riff

Guitar tuned down one step (low to high: D G C F A D)
All notes sound one step lower than written

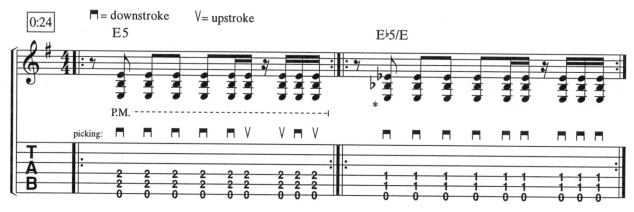

*Pick this section with muscle.

Diagram 32:
Open E5 Power Chord

Diagram 33:
E♭5/E chord

"**Example 83** is the single-note riff that ends the verse. It uses string bends and releases to add color to it and starts with a sinister-sounding move from E to F."

Example 83: "5 Minutes Alone" end of verse riff
Guitar tuned down one step (low to high: D G C F A D)
All notes sound one step lower than written

"**Example 84** is the pre-chorus riff, and it has some single-note stuff happening that involves finger slides and frantic left-hand vibrato. Rex [bass] really pulls a lot on making songs complete, and this riff is a good example of him doing that. When we were working on this tune, something was definitely missing just before the chorus and, like always, out of nowhere, Rex goes, 'How about adding this?' Then he played this riff off the top of his head that was perfect to complete the song. He took the weight off my back and made it shot time again! That's why we call Rex the Pit Boss."

Example 84: "5 Minutes Alone" pre-chorus riff
Guitar tuned down one step (low to high: D G C F A D)
All notes sound one step lower than written

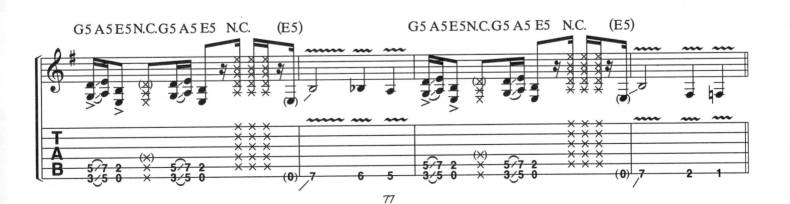

77

More Meandering Madness

"**Example 85** is the long-assed meandering riff that immediately follows the second chorus," Dime reports, playing the song's middle 8.

Example 85: "5 Minutes Alone" middle-8 riff
Guitar tuned down one step (low to high: D G C F A D)
All notes sound one step lower than written

As you can see, the first four bars of **Example 85** are very similar to the first meandering run we looked at in **Example 81**. In fact, bars 2 and 4 are identical to it, with bars 1 and 3 featuring a slight variation. Observation over—back to Dime.

"We then go straight into another single-note-based riff that combines slides, chromatic shit and tritone intervals," says Darrell, referring to the second half of the passage, bars 5–8. "At the very end of this run I use power chords to add fatness and a downhill chromatic slide to make the riff avalanche right back into the main jam (Example 86). This time around, though, the main riff goes half as long with a trick fill added in the middle (trip-a-let, trip-a-let, trip-a-let, ching) and finishes with a low-E-string bar-dump."

Example 86: "5 Minutes Alone" pre-solo riff

Guitar tuned down one step (low to high: D G C F A D)
All notes sound one step lower than written

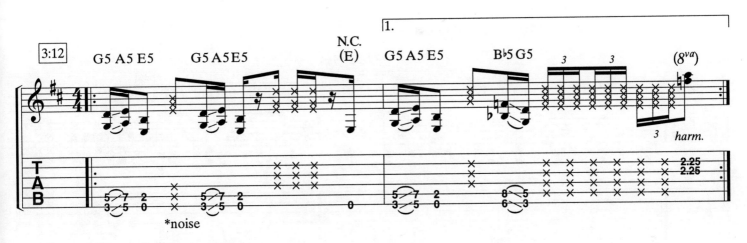

*noise

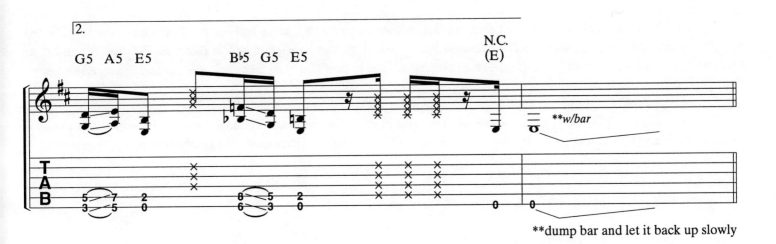

**dump bar and let it back up slowly

Ass Stomp!

"Last, let's scope out **Example 87,** which is the 'Ass Stomp!' breakdown riff that happens after the solo, which we'll look at lata—I promise [Note: the solo is discussed in **Chapter 9**]. This riff features two dark intervals that we scoped out in 'Evil Intervals' [**Chapter 6**]: the lowered fifth [E5 to B♭5 and vice versa] and the minor second [E5 to F5]. It also has a power-chord slide happening [F5 to G5] and calls on you to mute the strings with both hands between the chords to make the riff sound tight and abrupt and keep the holes of silence clean. Remember, loose is cool sometimes, but for this riff, tight and abrupt is where it's at."

Example 87: "5 Minutes Alone" "Ass Stomp!" riff

Guitar tuned down one step (low to high: D G C F A D)
All notes sound one step lower than written

"Watch out with this riff though, 'cos at the very end comes the curve ball—a 6/4 bar that repeats the E5-F5-E5-F5-G5 section that finishes the previous bar [marked as the 'two-beat riff' in **Example 87**] twice and then ends with some fast, percussive muted-string chucking. This brings the 'Ass Stomp!' section to an aggressive climax that slams into the final chorus.

"I hope you've been able to use some of this crap in your own playing. Although this is the way I play these riffs, if anything feels awkward, do it your own way and keep 'em rollin'. Stay loose, stay driven, keep your amps overdriven and flat-ass, straight-out jam!"

Chapter 8

"I hate guys who play fast leads all the time just because they can. C'mon, slow down and play some notes that count, dude. Hell, I'll take one note over a million any day! Play that one note with heart, feel and guts and then let that sucker sing, just like Billy Gibbons does. Hey, don't get me wrong, I love wailing out leads as much as the next guy BUT only if it complements the track. And sometimes that means not taking a solo. I don't wanna come off like I'm trying to take away from playing lead, 'cos I play ****in' lead, man! I've worked real hard on my technique, and it comes from the heart, y'know. To me though, playing what works best for the song is much more important than trying to impress other guitarists by jerking off all over the neck or showing off your new three-handed guitar technique. If the track calls for it, then I'll rip, BUT if I feel that only one or two notes played from the gut will do the trick, then that's exactly what I'll do. I certainly don't feel an obligation to try to prove my chops every time I take a lead—tone and feel are much more important.

"My lead in '5 Minutes Alone' is a good example of what I'm talking about here. I remember the relearning process of 'simple is hard to beat' when it came to the solo in that song! I was struggling to play something way too involved in way too short a lead space. Then, all of a sudden I saw the right light for this section—I got on one note and never got off. To me that's all it took. If it was a snake, it would've bit me!

"Sure, you can express yourself by stepping out as a lead player, but it's always truly something to see a live band jam together on a riff and hump it and ride it—that's impressive right there, regardless of what type of music they're playing. We do that kind of shit a lot. When we work a riff, it's not a lead break, it's a band break. For example, there's a part in 'War Nerve' that was originally gonna have a lead break over it, but we weren't happy with the section I was supposed to solo over. Then, while we were working on improving the part under the lead, we came up with a riff idea that kicked so damned hard we went, '**** the lead, let's ride on this instead—it'll kill when we jam on it live!' Basically, provided it's a bad-assed part, you're not gonna miss having the lead there. Pantera's a machine, and when we all throw down on a wicked part, it sounds real ****in' tough!"

Dimebag Darrell

As stated in the **Introduction**, Dime is one of the few players who rose to prominence in the '90s who not only plays lead guitar but positively blazes at it! Hence the reason he's graced countless guitar magazine covers and won so many Best Hard Rock/Heavy Metal Guitarist readers' polls. As the above quote clearly shows though, Dime never has thrown and never will throw a mind-boggling lead break into a song just because he can. First and foremost, he's a team player—a stance he'll make perfectly clear (if he hasn't already!) later on in this chapter.

This said, as already stated, he truly is a phenomenal soloist. So, without further ado, let's explore a few of his lead-playing traits. As was the case in **Chapter 6**, certain topics are dealt with via Dime answering a *Riffer Madness* reader's letter. We're gonna begin by learning Dime's thoughts on "learning from others, wide-assed left-hand stretches, symmetrical runs and the importance of your pinky."

Stretches From Hell

"Some dudes tend to get intimidated whenever they come across a guy who really rips on guitar, but not me, man—I get inspired," Darrell tells us. "As far as I'm concerned, playing ain't a competition. Hearing someone smoke always lights my fire and makes me try out new ideas and learn new shit. I don't sit down with a pile of records and try to cop licks though. What I'm into is checking the dude's overall playing vibe and learning from that. Use your ears and learn all that you can from anything. Listen!

"When I first started out, one of my biggest influences was Eddie Van Halen—the stuff he did on the first two Van Halen albums was so aggressive and ballsy-sounding, it still gives me chills. Anyway, I kept seeing pictures in *Guitar World* of him doing big-assed left-hand finger stretches, and that inspired me to start dicking around with some wide-stretch ideas of my own—like the two E-minor licks shown in **Example 88** and **Example 89**. Another thing I learned from studying those pictures was the importance of my little finger. It's there, so use it—it definitely gives you more reach!"

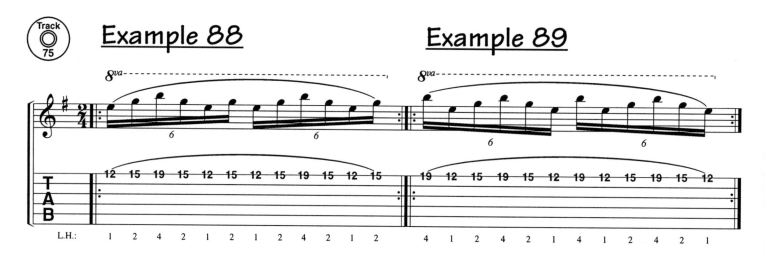

Awkwardly Cool Runs

"As I got to know my guitar neck better, I realized that there was an E note at the 10th fret on the A string—how 'bout that?! Then, when I was jamming around one day, I thought to myself, 'Hey! I know some wide-stretch E-minor licks on the high-E string that start on the E note at the 12th fret and also use the 19th fret. So, why don't I try moving one of these fingering-pattern ideas across each string in turn until I finish up on the E note at the 19th fret on the A string?' **Example 90** shows me applying this concept to the lick we looked at in **Example 89**."

Example 90

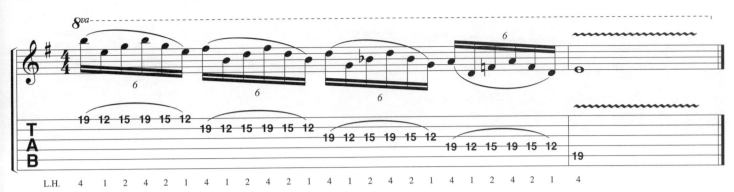

```
L.H.  4  1  2  4  2  1  4  1  2  4  2  1  4  1  2  4  2  1  4  1  2  4  2  1  4
```

IMPORTANT PLAYING NOTE: When performing such wide-stretch lead passages, Dime invariably adopts a "classical" playing position with his left (fretboard) hand (LH)—namely with his LH thumb at the back of the neck (see **Photo 1**) as opposed to having it anchored over the upper edge of the fretboard (see **Photo 2**) in the typical "rock lead" manner. By placing his LH thumb at the back of the neck, Dime is able to maximize the wideness of his fretboard stretch. Try it and you'll see what I mean.

Photo 1: "Classical" LH Position

Photo 2: Typical "Rock" LH Position

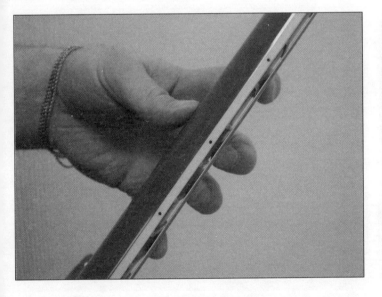

"Since the fingering pattern in **Example 90** is exactly the same on each string, a lot of guys call this kind of thing a *symmetrical run*," Dime informs us. "It's simple, but cool. To be honest with you, I have no idea what the hell scales this run uses because I'm not a cat that's heavy on theory. All I know is that it sounds awkwardly cool in the key of E minor and that's all that matters. Listen closely and let your ears decide what notes are right or wrong! Feel and spontaneity are my bag; you don't have to be a music-theory genius to come up with cool-sounding ideas. Just play something like you mean it and you'll be fine—whether you understand what's going on or not! Anyhow, because this idea worked, I got into futzing around with symmetrical runs in a major way.

"**Example 91** is another example of a wide-stretch symmetrical run in E minor and is kinda similar to the one I do near the start of my 'Cowboys From Hell' solo. How I came up with this ascending passage was real simple. I was messing around with a wide-stretch lick on the low E string [indicated as the 'initial lick' in **Example 91**] and figured, 'Hey, let's see what happens if I take this pattern right across the neck and end up on the high E string.' I tried it, it sounded cool as shit, and so I used it in my 'Cowboys' lead. Once again, I have absolutely no clue what's happening scale-wise—to me it's just a ripping E-minor run that works!"

Example 91

Track 77

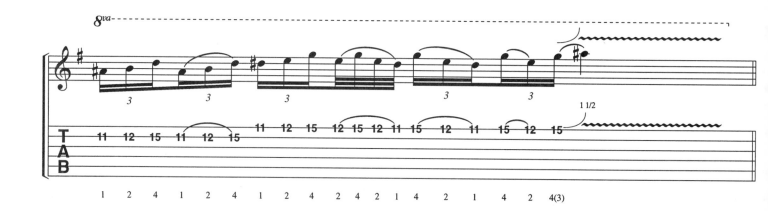

To aid you in your visualization of the symmetrical fingering pattern Dime is referring to here, **Diagram 34** shows a fretboard diagram of the fingering pattern **Example 91** uses.

Diagram 34

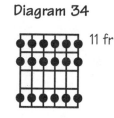

11 fr

Example 92 depicts another E minor-based symmetrical run from the vast repertoire of our subject. In fact, it's a lick he showed me way back in 1990 when I conducted my first-ever *Guitar World* piece on Dime, which was aptly titled "The Guitar Lesson From Hell!" The fact that it is built on septuplets (seven evenly spaced notes per beat) gives it a graceful, lilting quality. This particular run requires a goodly amount of left-hand strength and accuracy (especially in the pinky) due to its wide stretches, fast slides and legato (smooth) nature. Pace yourself sensibly for this one by starting off slowly. And, as Dime has already pointed out earlier in this book, "If you're not used to using your pinky a lot or doing these kinds of wide-stretch runs, then please do yourself a favor—always warm up your fingers before you go for broke. If you don't, you could tool your hands off and that would suck big-time!"

Once again, to help you visualize the symmetry involved, **Diagram 35** shows the fingering pattern involved.

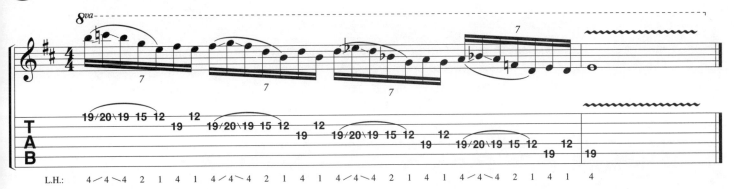

Example 92

Track 78

Diagram 35

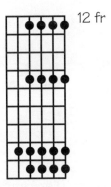

12 fr

"Try creating some wide-stretch symmetrical runs of your own, and never be afraid to try something out. Just go for it, dude," Darrell concludes. "Hell, if what you come up with sucks, just C-section it and move onto something else! I know the idea behind these runs is simple, but who gives a shit—as we've just seen, the results can sound bad-assed. So keep on jamming and stay hard, damn it! Timbale!"

Go Wide

Dear Darrell,
I think it's great how you use parts of your songs to make points in your lesson. After listening to "This Love," I'm curious how you control such wide bends. I tried to figure it out but was unsuccessful.

Jake Hotop
Centerville, VA

"To be accurate when you're doing big-assed string bends like the ones in 'This Love,' you've gotta use your ears, man—it's all a matter of pitch. Another thing that'll help give you more control over your bending is using more than one finger to do the bend. For example, when I bend a note with my little finger, I help it out with my other three fingers too [see **Photo 3**]. The guys at *Guitar World* tell me that the correct term for this technique is *reinforced bending*."

Photo 3: Reinforced Bending

One Fret at a Time

Howdy Dude,

I'm completely blown away with your sound and technique and, like any guitarist, I wish I could do more on the fretboard than I can. Just like you though, I'm a spazzer who can't sit down for shit and teach myself scales and things—I just like to jam! Are there any tricks of the trade you know that could give me some new lead ideas?

Wayne "Farm Boy" Farmer
Arlington, TX

"One word, Farm Boy—chromatics. I think a lot of people are real intrigued by all those different modes and shit, whereas I'm kinda more inclined to take a lick and then try moving it up or down the neck chromatically [i.e., one fret at a time]. It's the simplest thing in the world to do and it can sound killer! Try it, man. Sit there and burn a lick like the simple A-minor one shown in the first bar of **Example 93**. Then, start moving it chromatically up the fretboard [toward the bridge] like in bars 2 and 3. Although I take this lick up a whole octave [12 frets], you don't have to do that—you can start and stop wherever you like 'cos, for the millionth time in *Riffer Madness*, there are no rules! Moving a lick chromatically down the neck [toward the nut] works real well too."

Example 93

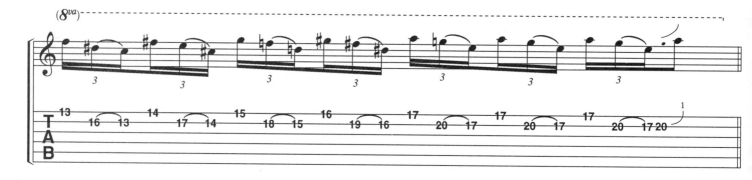

Pinky Power Revisited

Darrell,

I saw you guys play recently (killer show!) and it looked like you use your pinky one hell of a lot. I haven't been playing too long, and whenever I use mine the tip of it hurts like hell. I'll work on it though, if you think it'll make me be able to play better. Thanks, man. Later.

Richard Preusse
Munich, Germany

"I'd definitely advise you to use your pinky, bro—I use mine all the time. On stretch licks you gotta have it in there, and it comes in real handy when you're jamming out riffs on the low E and A strings too—like the 'Shedding Skin' one we checked out earlier in **Example 28** in **Chapter 6**. If you don't use your pinky much, try throwing it in there 'cos you might come up with something cool that you've never done before. I mean, the A-minor blues lick shown in **Example 94** would be pretty tough to play if you didn't use your pinky. Using your little finger definitely opens up the neck some more, so why limit yourself? Don't be one of those people that goes, 'Oh my pinky's weak—I ain't gonna use it.' It's there, so why not use the ****er!"

Example 94

To Lead or Not to Lead? That Is the Question

Hey Dime,
Pantera is my favorite band and you're definitely my favorite guitarist—you rule, bro! Now that I'm done ass-kissing, here's my question. I dig your lead-playing big-time and was wondering why you don't do a solo in every song—like in "Slaughtered" for instance. What's the deal?

Eddie Gray
Leeds, England

"I love playing lead but only when it fits the vibe of the song, and sometimes a cut just doesn't need a solo! I try to look more at the big picture—by trying to figure out what's appropriate for the tune. 'Slaughtered' is a good example of what I'm talking about here. When we were working on that song, at first we decided that we were gonna insert a slow, melodic lead part into the middle of it. But while we were working on that slow section, everyone was just kinda sippin' on their beers and staying real quiet. Then I stepped back and realized that because of the slow section, the tune had lost its momentum and power, so I said, '**** the lead!' The big picture, man, that's where it's at."

Sussing Out Harmony Leads

Dear Dimebag,
Your column is cool and helps me out a lot. Could you please talk about harmony solos, like the one in "Hollow" [Vulgar Display of Power]. Harmony solos kick ass and I don't know how to figure them out. If you could explain how you do 'em, it'd really help me. Lata!

Lance Perkins
Evesham, England

"Jacking around with a tape machine and trying to come up with harmony leads opened up a whole new world for me when I was growing up. I'd record a single-note line like the simple one in A minor shown in **Example 95** and then play it back and work out the harmony to it."

Example 95

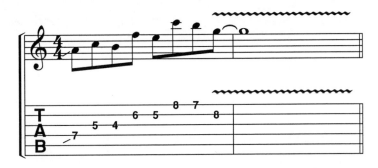

"You don't have to have a fancy-assed four-track machine to do this either; a shitty old boom box with a built-in condenser mike will work just fine—hell, that's how I used to do it! Also, because I didn't have a drum machine to keep time by, I'd just record my floor-tapping so I'd have something to go by when I was listening to playback.

"When I'm working out a harmony part, I usually start off by playing the exact same lick three frets higher up the neck [i.e., a minor third higher] instead of trying to use any knowledge of theory, which is next to nothing anyway! When you do this, most of the harmony notes you'll play will work, but there are usually two or three that sound wrong. Fixing the harmony notes that don't sound right is easy, man. You can start by just scooting each one of those bad boys one fret higher up the neck [this will make the harmony-line note a major third (i.e., three tones) higher than the original note] and then see how that sounds. Then, if some of those notes still bug you, try moving 'em somewhere else until it all sounds good to you. There are a bunch of different intervals that can sound good depending on what you're looking for. Like I'm always saying to ya—use your ears!

"To show you what I mean, let's suss out a harmony line to **Example 95** using this approach. First, get your foot tapping and record the run [hint: give yourself a 'one, two, three, four' count-in with your foot before you start playing so that you'll know exactly when the recorded lick starts on playback]. Then rewind the tape and see what it sounds like when you double it with the exact same lick played three frets higher, as in **Example 96**."

Note: To help you hear what Dime is getting at here, on the CD track **Example 95** is panned hard left (LHS) and **Example 96** is panned hard right (RHS).

Example 96

(RHS of stereo on CD track, LHS = **Example 95**)

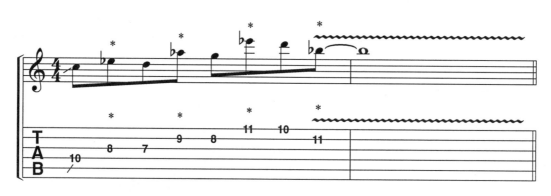

✳ = see text

"To my ears, the harmonies to the first, third, fifth and seventh notes in the run sound cool, and the ones to the second, fourth, sixth and eighth notes [marked with an '✳' above **Example 96**] don't. So, let's scoot those four bad harmony notes up a fret like in **Example 97** and try again. Now the whole thing sounds right. Geddit? Once again, it's simple shit that works."

Note: Once again, on the CD track **Example 95** is panned hard left (LHS) and **Example 97** is panned hard right (RHS).

Example 97

(RHS of stereo on CD track, LHS = **Example 95**)

"**Example 98** is the first two bars of the main lead guitar part [Gtr 1: LHS of stereo] that opens up 'Hollow' [*Vulgar Display of Power*] and **Example 99** [Gtr 2: RHS of stereo] is the accompanying harmony line. Before you check out **Example 99** though, see if you can work it out by yourself by using the ideas we just rapped about."

Note: to help you hear how these two lines complement each other, on the CD track **Example 98** is panned hard left (LHS) and **Example 99** is panned hard right (RHS).

Example 98: "Hollow" intro harmony line

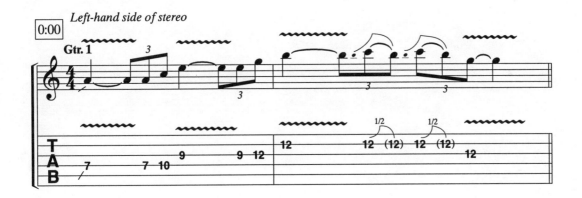

Example 99: "Hollow" intro harmony line

89

The Mindset Behind the "Cemetary Gates" Solo

Dear Dime,

Thanks to a killer transcription of "Cemetary Gates" that appeared in Guitar World, I've nailed the solo and my band now plays the song live. Of course, our version isn't as good as yours, but it still kicks ass and the crowd loves it! Of all your solos, that one is my all-time favorite. So, my question is not how you play it but how you came up with that lead—did you work it out or did you just wing it?

Chris Jett
Charlotte, NC

"Thinkin' back, this story has got a cool little twist to it. Check it out—I remember knowing I needed to come up with something cool and bad-assed leadwise for 'Cemetary Gates.' So one night I'd been out partyin' hard, jammin' to music, boozin' and what-not. When I got home I had a good buzz-on from the evening and I was still thinkin' 'Cemetary' lead, 'Cemetary' lead! So, I went straight out to my four-track room, picked up my axe and cranked it loud as hell with the loose buzz theory that anything and everything goes—JUST PLAY! I hit 'record' and played three solos back to back, not stopping to listen back to any of them.

"I wasn't too happy with what I'd done so I crashed out, passed out and woke up the next day thinking I had a lot of work to do. I almost started from scratch but then decided to slow down, take a moment and listen. So I fired up the four-track, put my ears [headphones] on and bam! Lo and behold, there it was! The first lead I played the night before was it for sure! Hey, man, the second and third takes weren't bad, but #1 had that first take magic so I didn't touch it!"

Chapter 9

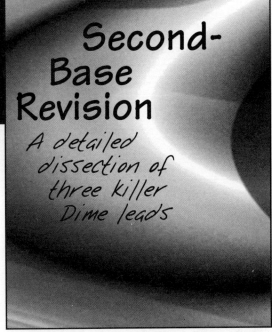

Second-Base Revision

A detailed dissection of three killer Dime leads

In this fun-filled chapter we're gonna burn through no fewer than three classic Dime solos note for note: "I'm Broken" and "5 Minutes Alone" from *Far Beyond Driven* plus the outro lead from "Floods" [*The Great Southern Trendkill*]. So, as Dime would no doubt say, crank your amp and get ready to bust a nut! This said, I'm gonna once again hand you over to the man with the purple goatee and the signed Ace Frehley tattoo on his chest.

Solo 1: "5 Minutes Alone" (live version)

"What's up, bro! As previously promised [in **Chapter 7**], we're gonna zone in on the '5 Minutes Alone' solo. Since I used two guitars on the recording, I'm gonna show you the one-guitar version that I play live. If you have problems nailing this right off the bat, try breaking it down into sections and then focus on one chunk at a time. Go slow until you get it right and then work it up to speed."

Example 100 shows the solo in question in its entirety. As a means of following Dime's sensible "break it down into sections" suggestion, it has been divided into six bite-sized licks as marked above the example.

Example 100: "5 Minutes Alone" solo (live version)

Track 85

Guitar tuned down one step (low to high: D G C F A D)
All notes sound one step lower than written

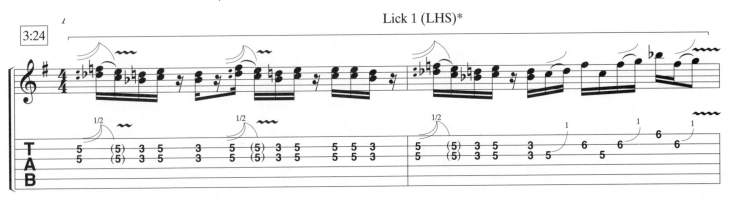

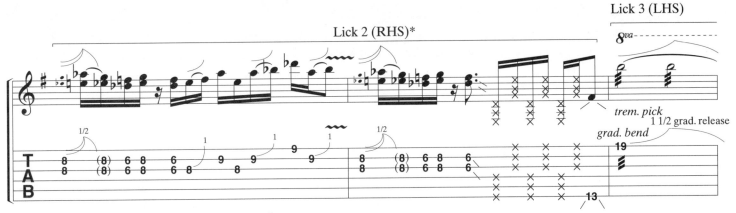

*LHS = Left-hand side of stereo mix.
RHS = Right-hand side of stereo mix.

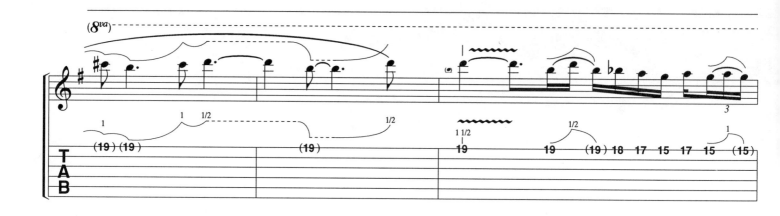

Lick 4 (RHS)

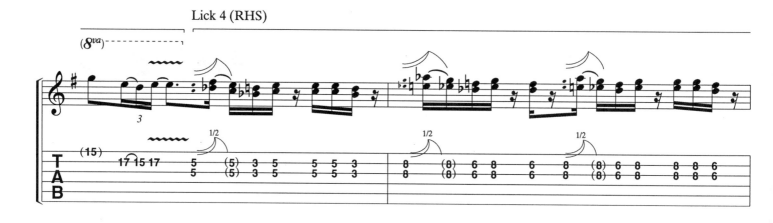

Lick 5 (LHS)

*Sound open string, drop bar, hit harmonic indicated and then use bar to pull harmonic up to pitch indicated.

**See Chapter 10 for detailed description and lessons on Dime's trademark "Harmonic Screams" technique.

"The solo starts off with a bluesy doublestop lick in G," Dime continues, playing the section of **Example 100** marked Lick 1. "I barre the B and G strings at the 5th fret with my ring finger and then bend 'em both up about a half-step. I kinda look at this as bending a small piece of a C5 power chord. I do this bend by pushing the B and G strings up toward the thicker strings, but you can also do it by pulling 'em down toward the floor. Either method will work, so try both ways and go with the one that works best for you.

"Bar 3 is the exact same lick as the one in bar 2 but moved up the neck three frets [Lick 2]. Then, at the beginning of bar 5, we get into milking one note for all it's worth! All I basically do for the next three bars is tremolo-pick the shit out of the B note at the 19th fret on the high-E string while bending and releasing it as shown [Lick 3]. On the record it kinda sounds like a siren going off because of the doubling. You can kinda get this effect on one guitar by adding a tight slap-back echo or some loose chorus, since you obviously can't play two guitars at once—even if you use your third arm!

"In bars 8 and 9 I hit a short E-minor blues run (E, G, A, B♭, B, D) and then dive back into the bluesy theme that started the solo off [Lick 4]. To bring the whole thing to a climax, I move this lick up the neck to A♯ in bar 10 and then C in bar 11 [Lick 5] before finishing D in bar 12. I close the whole thing with a harmonic squeal, where I use the whammy bar to pull the natural harmonic that lies a hair behind the 2nd fret on the G string up to the pitch of D [Lick 6].

"If you don't play much lead, don't peak out. This is the perfect simplistic lead to get you off the ground and into soloing. You can do it, damn it, so let it fly—you've got it! For you more advanced players, I got some good shit brewing up for you, so hold tight!"

Solo 2: The Broken Break!

Next up, Dime walks us through his excellent "I'm Broken" lead. He starts off by taking a close-up look at the six licks that make up the first nine bars of this attention-grabbing solo. Once again, these six bite-sized licks are clearly marked above the excerpt, which is shown in **Example 101** below. So tune your axe down a whole-step (low to high: D, G, C, F, A, D) and let's cut right to the chase.

Example 101: The First Nine bars of the "I'm Broken" Solo

Guitar tuned down one step (low to high: D G C F A D)
All notes sound one step lower than written

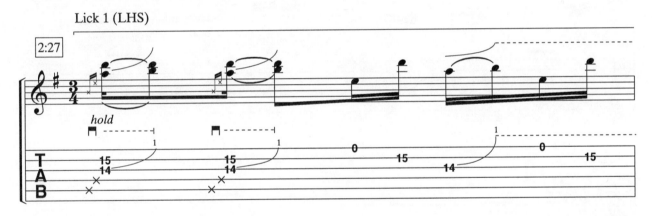

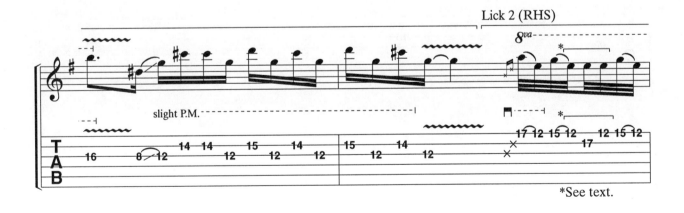

*See text.

Lick 2 continued

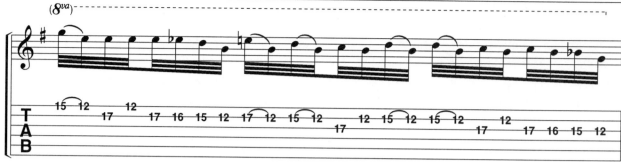

Lick 2 continued

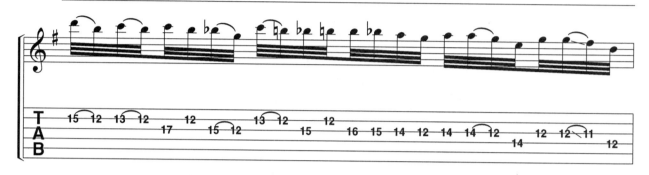

Lick 3 (LHS)　　　　　　　　　　　　　　　　Lick 4 (RHS)

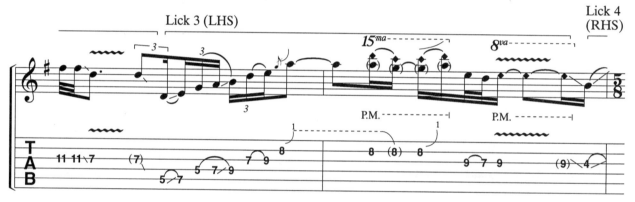

Lick 4 continued

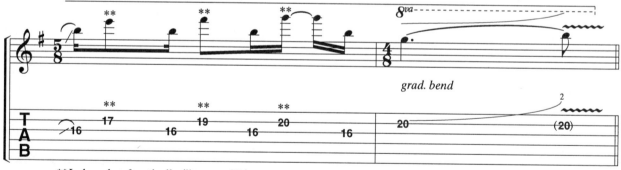

**Jerk up bar frantically (listen to CD).

"This solo is in E minor and starts off with me muting the A and D strings with my left-hand index finger and doing a big rake across 'em for maximum attack," Dime reveals. "The first lick we jam out [Lick 1] is pretty straightforward: Hit the notes at the 14th fret on the G string and the 15th fret on the B string together and let 'em both ring while you bend the G-string note up a whole-step to B. Do this twice and then add the open high-E-string note as indicated and let it ring too. Sure, this riff is pretty simple, but it's a cool and effective way to get the solo cookin'.

"In bar 2 we hit a lick [Lick 2] that keeps going back to the G note at the 12th fret on the G string. This kinda thing is called a pedal point lick because I'm pedaling around the same note. Notice that I lightly mute the strings with the palm of my picking hand when I play this to make the notes jump out a tad more.

"At the end of bar 3, we get into a long, winding, wide-stretch symmetrical run [Lick 3] that is chromatic up-the-ass. A lot of dudes probably wouldn't play this particular lick because it doubles up on a bunch of notes—they'd want to keep hitting different notes to make the passage descend better. To me though, the run's fine, man! It's trick-sounding and there's nothing wrong with hitting the same note a few times before movin' on. Besides, when a note is repeated in this lick, it's played on a different string each time and that makes it sound slightly different. Let's scope out the first time this happens at the end of bar 3 [marked with an asterisk (*)].

"Here an E note is played three times in succession: the first and third ones are played at the 12th fret on the high string, but the middle one is at the 17th fret on the B string. Compare these two E notes and you'll hear that they do sound a little different. I finish this symmetrical run with a short, double-picked descending lick [Lick 4] on the G and D strings. Then, straight after that we go into a short, ascending sliding run [Lick 5] that finishes with a pick-induced harmonic squeal on a bend.

"The next thing I do in this solo is slide up the neck and do a short lick [Lick 6] that pedals around the B note at the 16th fret on the G string. Also, each time I play a note on the B string in the first bar of this lick [the three notes in question are each marked by two asterisks (**)], I jerk my whammy bar up real quick. Listen to the CD [2:44–2:46] and you'll hear exactly what I'm doin' there. This lick finishes off with a two-step bend at the 20th fret on the B string, and we're gonna zone closely on that 'cos how you do this bend is real important to the next part of the solo. I've seen transcriptions that say I use a DigiTech Whammy Pedal to do this lick, but it's not true! All I'm doing is bending the shit out of two notes at the same time—the note at the 20th fret of the B string and the note at the 20th fret of the G string too. Here's how you do it."

Warped Two-String Bending From Hell!

"When you bend the B-string note at the end of this lick [Lick 6] you've gotta let the D string slide under your left-hand (LH) fingers so that when you come back down, you've got hold of both strings at the 20th fret. Then, for the next two bars all you do is bend and release both strings together before finishing the lick with a one-and-a-half-step bend at the end of the 21st fret on the high-E string. This particular lick looks a shitload more difficult written out in tabulature than it really is, so listen carefully to the album and catch what's going on that way.

"Nailing this two-string bending technique might take a while because, normally, when you bend a note on the B string, your bending fingers push the G string out of the way and keep it off the fretboard so it stays quiet. For this lick though, you've gotta flatten out your bending fingers so the G string can get under 'em—kinda like a two-string barre with wicked bends [double-stop bending]. Don't worry about being exact with these bends either, man—they're supposed to sound warped and ****ed up!

"The solo finishes with the lick shown in **Example 102** [2:54–3:04], a straightforward symmetrical pattern on the B and high-E strings that climaxes with a chromatic climb up the high E followed by a one-step bend at the 22nd fret."

Example 102: The Last Three Bars of the "I'm Broken" Solo
Guitar tuned down one step (low to high: D G C F A D)
All notes sound one step lower than written

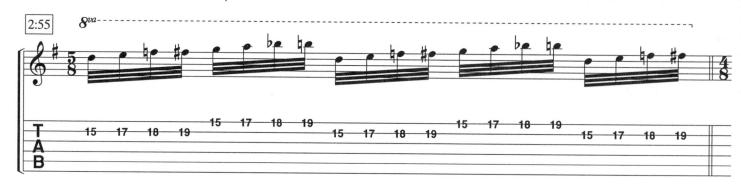

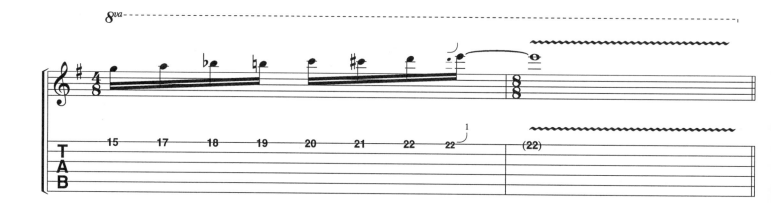

"Now that you've got the map, the knowledge and the tools to play this solo, try working it up to speed and jamming it with the record," Dime concludes. "This is how I used to get my nut. It's ****in' fun!"

Solo 3: The "Floods" Outro
This particular piece is a personal favorite of mine for three reasons:
1) It sounds great (duh!).
2) It is relatively easy to play.
3) As you'll discover later, I was kinda, sorta involved in this piece making it on the album.

While the vast majority of Dime's playing is based on his unique blend of viciousness and virtuosity, some of his most memorable moments are surprisingly soulful and mellow. Take his soaring, emotion-soaked solo in "10's" or his stunning solo in the band's killer cover of Sabbath's "Planet Caravan," which appears on *Far Beyond Driven*. The former is something Gary Moore would no doubt be proud of, and even though the latter lead break is completely devoid of distortion (gasp!), it's been a show-stopping highlight of countless Pantera gigs.

Not surprisingly then, Dime's melodic and moody outro to the song "Floods" is one of the most requested "how the hell do I play that?" passages from the *Trendkill* album. This hauntingly catchy piece of wide-stretch arpeggiation is shown in **Example 103**.

Example 103: "Floods" Outro Solo

Guitar tuned down one step (low to high: D G C F A D)
All notes sound one step lower than written

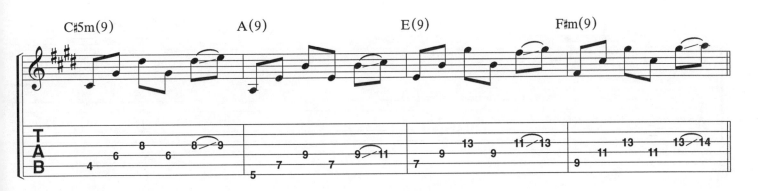

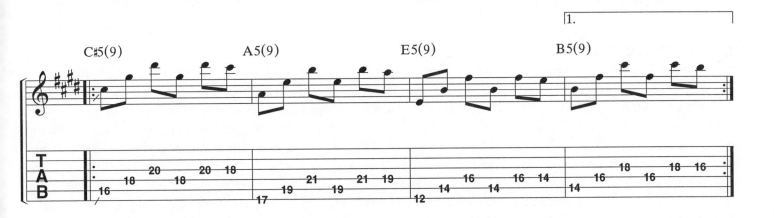

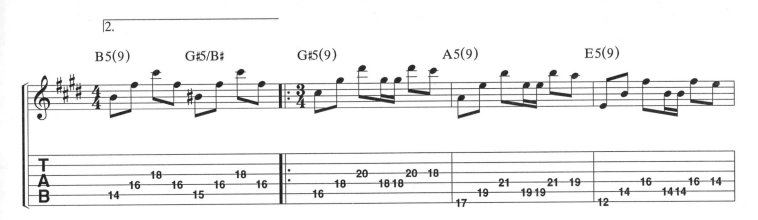

continued→

Example 103 *(continued)*

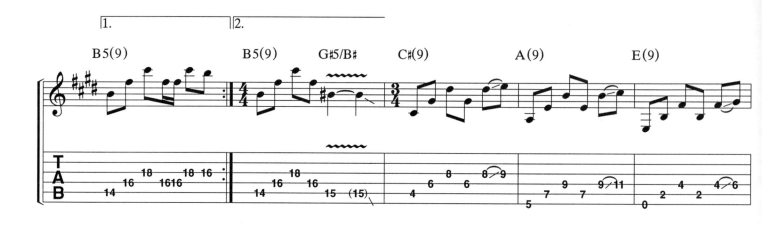

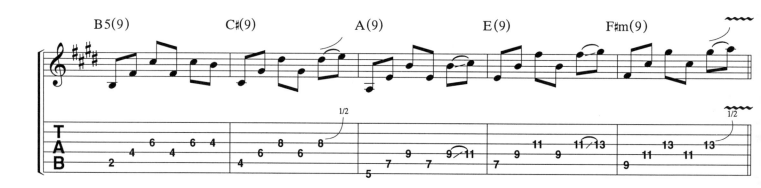

Before we get into the nitty-gritty of how to play this neat little part, let's check out the story behind how it made it onto the album because it's quite a tale.

How the "Floods" Outro Solo Was Recorded

It was about 5:30 in the morning and I was pulling an all-nighter, working on a crunch deadline for the Dimebag "Destroyer! Pantera Returns" cover story for the June 1996 issue of *Guitar World*. I was busy transcribing the tapes of the lengthy interviews I'd just done with Dime up at Camp Strapped when the phone rang. "What jack-off would call at this time of the morning?" I thought to myself as I hit the pause button of my tape machine and listened as my answering machine picked up. To my amazement, the voice I heard coming from the phone was the same exact one I'd been transcribing—it was Dime! Needless to say, I took the call.

"Nicholas Cage [as revealed in the "What's In a Name?" section in **Chapter 2**—Darrell's big on nicknames], I'm sorry to call you at such a ****ed-up time, but I need your help," Dime blurted. "We're in New York mastering the album and I need to re-cut a part first thing in the morning. Trouble is, I don't have any of my shit with me. Is there any way you can get a guitar and a G1 to me by 9 a.m. today?" I took down Dime's hotel number and the studio address and promised him I'd do everything I could to make it happen. Trouble was, I'm a lefty so one of my axes wouldn't cut it, and I didn't have a G1 at home either.

I poured through my address book and luckily was able to track down the legendary Steve Pisani of Sam Ash on 48th Street, NY fame. Not only did Steve not mind my calling him at home (I was nice enough to wait until 7 a.m.!) at the crack of dawn, he stepped to the plate like the true champ he is. And, as a result, an axe (with the intonation correctly set up!) and a Korg G1 pedal were delivered to the mastering studio by 9 a.m. that morning. Thanx again for that, Mr. Pisani. You rule!

Now that the scene is set, I'm gonna pass you over to Dime, who will fill you in on the before and after of this unusual tale.

"This is a pretty good story even though I say it myself," laughs Dime. "What happened was this: I remember I was all jacked-up in the studio one night while we were recording 'Floods.' It was real late and I'd been working and drinking all night and I just really wanted to record that ending part that goes over the rain so I could hear how it worked with the song as a whole. So, I just grabbed this guitar that was lying in the corner and put it down on tape. The trouble was that the guitar I picked up was way out of strobe [intonation] and I remember it sounding kinda sour and messed-up when the part starts to go higher and higher up the neck. I carried on anyway so I could hear it, but I meant to go back later and replay the ****er on a strobed-out [intonated] guitar. Like a dick though, I forgot all about it until we flew into New York to master the album.

"We were sitting in the mastering suite in New York, and when I heard it I just plain freaked out. How could I let such a sour-sounding, outta-tune thing slip by? We were on a real tight deadline and it was real late at night, but I knew I had to redo it no matter what. So, we worked through the night and mastered pretty much everything except that one song. Then, when we split to get a few hours' sleep before finishing up, that's when I called you.

"First thing the next morning, a runner came into the studio with the loaner guitar and the Korg G1 you'd set up, and I went, 'Okay, I'm gonna record it straight to DAT and then we'll fly it in.' This dude from the record label was there and he was totally freaked out! His voice was all shaky and he went, 'You're gonna record a part while we're mastering? You can't do that, it's never been done and I have to have the thing finished immediately. There's a car waiting downstairs and its going to leave in 45 minutes with the mastered album to get it printed. You don't understand, it's the Elektra way—we have to have it right away.'

"I said, 'No dude, you don't understand! This is the Pantera way—whatever it takes.' That said, I set up my shit in another room and went to record the part, but this dickhead from the label had gotten me all stressed out. There I was, trying to record this laid-back, mellow part when I was anything but laid-back and mellow, so it just wasn't kicking. So I slugged back a few beers and a Blacktooth Grin or two [a Blacktooth Grin is Pantera's drink of choice and consists of a healthy shot or three of Crown Royal or Seagram's 7 whiskey with a tiny splash of Coke] and tried again. I plugged straight into the G1 and played the part two or three times direct to DAT. Then, I took it into the mastering room, got Vinnie to choose the one he liked the best and we flew it in. And the record company man got the finished thing on time. Goddamn, that's one hell of a story, even though I say it myself!"

How to Play the "Floods" Outro Solo

If you look closely at **Example 103**, you'll see that this solo is based almost entirely around one chord shape—the 5add9—which consists of the following notes: root, perfect fifth and the major ninth (the major second an octave up). **Diagram 36** and **Diagram 37** are chord diagrams of this shape. **Diagram 36** has the root note on the low-E string while **Diagram 37** has the root note on the A string.

Diagram 36

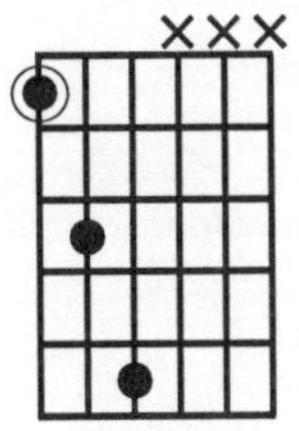

Diagram 37

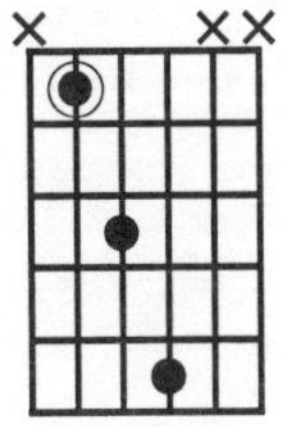

⊙ = root   ⊙ = root

If this chord sounds strangely familiar, it's because it's also the one used to create the memorable main riff of the huge Police hit, "Message in a Bottle."

Don't let the fact that the vast majority of this riff is in 3/4 time throw you—simply count "one-two-three, one-two-three" instead of "one-two-three-four" and you'll be there. The typical Dimebag wide-stretch nature of the 5add9 chord coupled with the fact that the passage also requires you to do quick one-fret or two-fret slides may well cause you problem as well, if you're not used to such playing. Don't fret though (sorry, bad pun!); to overcome these difficulties, just learn this solo by playing much slower than it appears on the album and *don't start speeding up* until you feel totally comfortable with it. Remember: *Slow but sure wins the race!*

Also, since this is a fairly lengthy passage, as we've already done with the two previous solos in the chapter, breaking it into bite-sized four-bar sections will probably help you master it that much quicker. Also, as you'll no doubt notice once you've played through it a few times, the piece does in fact contain a larger number of repeated passages with only very slight variations going on. So, don't let the apparent size of this passage alarm you—it's not as complex as it may first appear.

Last, but certainly not least, listening to the piece over and over until it becomes firmly fixed in your head might well prove to be helpful. As the saying goes: *If you can hum it, you can play it*—eventually! Good luck and have fun 'cos, ultimately, having fun is what playing the guitar is all about—period.

"Harmonics and a whammy bar? Those two things definitely go hand in hand if you ask me!"

Dimebag Darrell

In addition to writing great riffs and coming up with smokin' solos, Dime is also a demon when it comes to squeezing weird 'n' wonderful noises out of this axe. In this chapter Dime spills the beans on how he creates some of his trademark "noises"—like his creative Whammy pedal abuse during songs like "Becoming" (*Far Beyond Driven*) or the high-pitched "harmonic squeals" he uses to mimic Phil Anselmo's soulful screams at the climactic end of "Cemetary Gates." In fact, our very first topic is harmonics so, without further ado, let's get to it. Take it away, Dime.

Hell's Bells Part I: Get Natural

"Next up we're gonna talk about harmonics—how to get 'em, where you can find 'em and what you do with 'em. There are a number of different ways you can make harmonics happen. You can induce 'em with your pick [pinch harmonics—see **Chapter 6**], you can tap 'em like Eddie Van Halen does sometimes [tap or touch harmonics] or you can get 'em by lightly resting one of your left-hand fingers on a string and then picking it. The last type are called natural harmonics, and they're the suckers we're gonna be dicking with."

How

"The easiest place to get a natural harmonic on any string is at the 12th fret. All you do is lightly rest one of your left-hand fingers on a string directly above that fret and then pick it. Don't let the string touch the fret though, or it won't work, Dad! When you do this right, you'll hear a bell-like note that's exactly one octave higher than the open-string note. To help make harmonics easier to get, use your lead [bridge] pickup and a shitload of gain. When I first started experimenting with harmonics, I'd sometimes hook up two distortion boxes just to get my strings 'frying' 'cos that really helped bring out the harmonics. Also, once you've chimed the harmonic, it's not necessary to leave your finger on the string—in fact, if you let go of the string immediately after you pick it, the harmonic will ring twice as well."

Where

"You can also get harmonics happening above other frets like the 7th, 5th and 4th. Some dudes seem to think that these are the only points where harmonics happen but, as far as I'm concerned, there is literally a harmonic to be found at any place on any string. Check this out and you'll hear what I'm saying: Rest your left-hand bird finger [middle finger] lightly over the highest fret of your fat [low] E string, then start chugging out a groove on that string with your pick. While you're doing that, keep your left-hand finger resting lightly on the string and start moving it slowly toward the nut. You should hear a shit-load of different harmonics all over the string!

"Some of my favorite harmonics are actually located between frets. There are two really cool ones between the 2nd and the 3rd frets that I use a lot. One is at about a quarter of the way between the 2nd and 3rd frets, and the other is at about three quarters of the way. They're pretty hard to get, so once you find 'em make a mental note of exactly where they are.

"I use some pretty radical harmonics at the beginning of 'Heresy' [*Cowboys From Hell*]. **Example 104** shows this riff and, as you can see, it uses a bunch of harmonics on the low-E string. The best way to make sure you're playing this right is to listen to the record real carefully and then find the exact spots where all the harmonics are. Use your ears and your eyes, man—look and listen!"

Example 104: "Heresy" intro riff

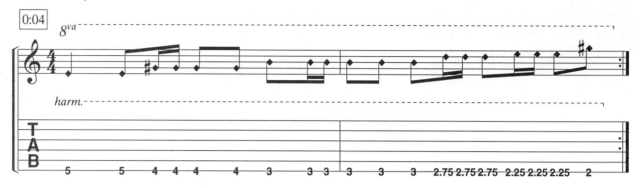

To Bar or Not to Bar

"A lot of guitarists tend to use only harmonics when they want to make weird noises with their whammy bars. That's cool but, as the intro to 'Heresy' shows, you don't need a tremolo arm to make harmonics wail. Two of my favorite players, Edward Van Halen and Randy Rhoads, both did some real happening things with harmonics without reaching for their bars! **Example 105** is the verse riff of "Mouth for War" [*Vulgar Display of Power*]. In bar 4, I play a simple little fill using harmonics a quarter of the way between the 2nd and 3rd frets on the G and B strings to create a high-pitched percussive sound that gives the riff an extra dimension. And, once again, no whammy-bar shit is going on."

Example 105: "Mouth for War" verse riff

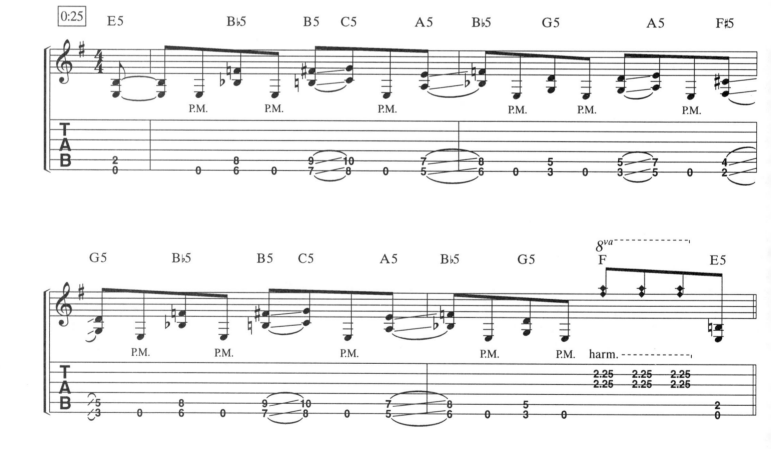

"Harmonics are cool to screw around with, so don't be afraid to experiment with 'em. Try, fail, live, learn—and die happy trying is my motto, bro! As long as you remember to *look* and *listen*, you'll do just fine. Next up I'm gonna tell ya all about how I get my trademark harmonic screams, like the ones at the end of 'Cemetery Gates.'"

Hell's Bells Part II: Harmonic Screams

'What's shakin', tough guy? As promised, I'm gonna light you up on how to do harmonic squeals. To get harmonic screams (same shit, different term!) happening, you need a whammy bar. So, if your axe doesn't have one, then you're gonna have to sit this section out—sorry, dude! Also, just so you know, we're gonna be doing some pretty brutal dives that will definitely knock a non-locking tremolo system way out of tune. So a locking one, like a Floyd Rose-type, is kind of essential.

"In case you're not exactly sure what I mean by a harmonic scream, there's a long, slow one in "This Love" that starts at 6:21 [CD time] and runs to the very end of the track. You can also hear me doing a bunch of them in 'Cemetery Gates', between 6:14 and the end, where I imitate Phil's screams. I love that sort of vocal stuff, but there's no way in hell I can do it in my voice—I don't have that kinda range! So, harmonic screams are my way of singing out, using my guitar instead of my throat—that's why I really dig this technique.

"I stumbled onto harmonic squeals when I was dicking around one day. A lot of people think I use a harmonizer or a [DigiTech] Whammy pedal to do them, but I don't; all I use is my bar and some natural harmonics. To make harmonics scream, I first dump my Floyd Rose real quick, hit a harmonic with my left hand while the string is still flapping and then use the bar to pull it up to the pitch I wanna hit.

"If this sounds kinda complex to you, don't schiz—it's actually a pretty simple thing to do once you've got the technique down. So, let's learn how to do a real basic harmonic scream in slow motion, by breaking the idea down into four easy steps. Let's use the harmonic that's directly above the 5th fret on the G string 'cos it's a pretty easy one to nail and make it scream up to its original pitch of G [**Example 106**]. First though, dial up a distorted sound [remember, gain helps harmonics happen] and switch to your lead [bridge] pickup."

Example 106

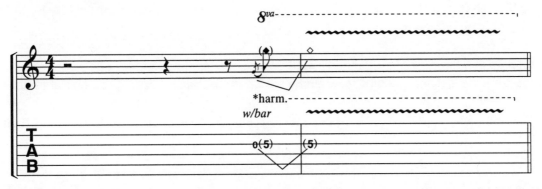

*Sound open note, drop bar, hit harmonic indicated and then return to pitch with bar as indicated.

"Now follow these steps:

➤ **Step 1:** Position your left hand so you're ready to hit the 5th-fret harmonic on the G string with your bird [middle] finger. Then mute the high E and B strings with your left-hand index finger, and the low E, A and D with your thumb by wrapping it around the top of neck.

➤ **Step 2:** Flick the G string with your bird finger and dump the bar down to the pitch you want the scream to start at. You can take the bar down as little or as far as you want; just don't take it down too far, or the string will die of shock and the harmonic won't happen.

➤ **Step 3:** As soon as the bar is dumped, sound the harmonic by lightly tapping the G string directly above the 5th fret with your bird finger. While you're doing this, make sure you're still keeping the other strings quiet with your thumb and index finger.

➤ **Step 4:** As soon as you've hit the harmonic, release pressure on the bar and let the G string return back up to pitch. As long as you've sounded the harmonic properly, it'll scream up to G [as shown in **Example 106**].

"The first few times you do this you're gonna hear the open G string growl before the scream starts happening. This is just because you're doing everything in slow motion. Once you've got this technique down though, you won't hear the growl because you'll be doing the first three steps so quickly they'll almost be simultaneous. If it takes you some time to get these squeals happening, don't skid—it took me a while too.

"Work on this technique until you can nail **Example 106** with no problem, then move onto **Example 107**. This one stays on the G string but has you screaming a bunch of different harmonics up to pitch. The last one can be a bitch to hit, but stick with it 'cos it sounds real cool when you nail it. Also, once you get this one down, try doing the same thing on the other five strings."

Example 107

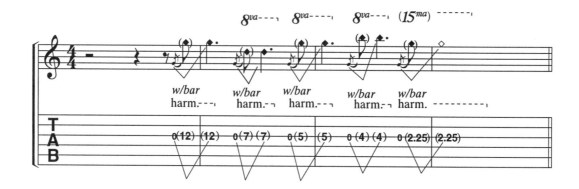

"Bust a nut on **Example 107** until you can nail it pretty much every time 'cos next up we'll be cranking these sons-of-bitches so high that dogs'll be barking! And while you're working on it, don't forget how ripped the guitar sounds, so get some of it, goddamn it!"

Squeal Like a Pig!
"What's up, Dad? So far we've got into using the whammy bar to make natural harmonics scream back up to pitch. Now we're gonna be using the bar to pull these jewels up to notes that are *higher* than their regular pitch—like screaming the harmonic at the 4th fret [regular pitch is B] on the G string all the way up to D as shown in **Example 108**."

Example 108

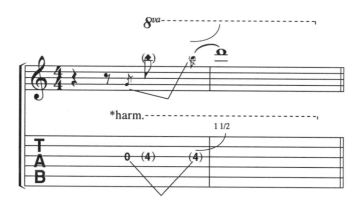

*Sound open string, drop bar, hit harmonic indicated
and then use bar to pull harmonic up to the pitch indicated.

"For you to be able to do this, your bridge needs to be floating [**Diagram 38**] so you can yank the bar up as well as push it down. It's up to you to decide how to set your bridge up but, just so you know, I have my Floyd set up so that I'm able to pull a note on the G string up about two-and-a-half steps."

Diagram 38: A "Floating" Tremolo Bridge

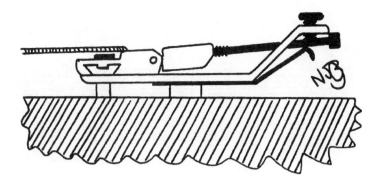

"Basically, the technique you need to get these high-pitched bastards screaming is exactly the same as the one we just talked about:

➤ **Step 1:** Flick the string with your left hand.

➤ **Step 2:** Dump the bar down.

➤ **Step 3:** Lightly tap the harmonic you want.

➤ **Step 4:** Let the whammy come back up real smoothly—so the harmonic squeals.

"The only difference is that this time you're gonna pull up on the bar so that the harmonic goes past its regular pitch and up to the note you want the scream to end on. To do this you've gotta use your ears as well as your hands—your hands do the work and your ears tell 'em how far to go."

Backward or Forward? The Choice Is Yours

"To pull a harmonic up to an exact pitch requires some pretty close control of the bar. I've found that with the bar pointing toward the back of my guitar [**Photo 4**] I can more accurately get to the note I'm aiming for because I have to push down on the bar to get there—think about it! But whenever I'm aiming for a gut-wrenching squeal, I go for it with the bar facing the front [**Photo 5**]. There's a different feel to both ways so experiment and find which one works best for you. Backward or forward? The choice is yours.

Photo 4: bar "facing the back"

Photo 5: bar "facing the front"

"Anyway, enough rapping about whammy bars and shit: let's get into doing some jamming. To get cooking on this new idea, check out **Example 109**. This has you screaming the harmonic at the 5th fret of the G string to four different notes: G (return to pitch); A (up a whole step); B (up two steps); and C (up two-and-a-half steps). I've got you hitting a power chord before each scream so you can hear the pitch you're aiming for just before you go for it with the harmonic. Use your ears and pay attention to the pitch."

Example 109

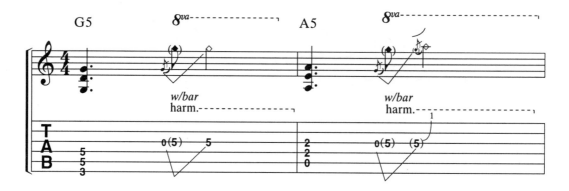

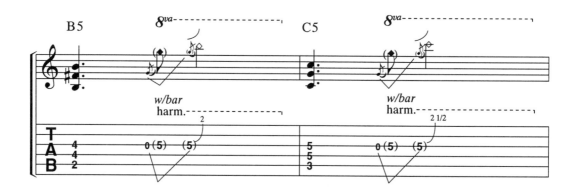

"Once you've got **Example 109** down, try **Example 110,** which is the same exact deal except without the power chords to help you out. This time you're flying blind!"

Example 110

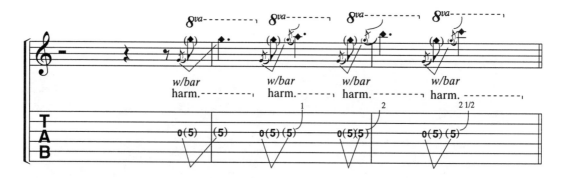

"Once you can nail **Example 110** every time, you're ready to start cutting up. Try squealing every harmonic you can find on every string, and never be afraid to experiment; that's how most of us come up with some of our coolest shit. The great thing about this technique is you can use it to make your guitar sing a melody or just squeal wildly outta control—it's up to you."

"To finish up, I'm gonna leave you with a challenge, **Example 111.** This is the first melodic squeal I do at the end of 'Cemetary Gates' [CD time: 6:20], where I follow Philip's vocal melody. Here I scream the harmonic at the 4th fret on the G string up to E, which is two-and-a-half steps above its resting pitch of B. Then, after holding it there for a measure, I drop it smoothly to C, which is a half-step above its resting pitch. The tough thing about this one is that you never get to use the harmonic's resting pitch (B) as a reference point—you're either above or below it, but never on it."

Track
96 ## Example 111: The first melodic squeal in "Cemetary Gates"

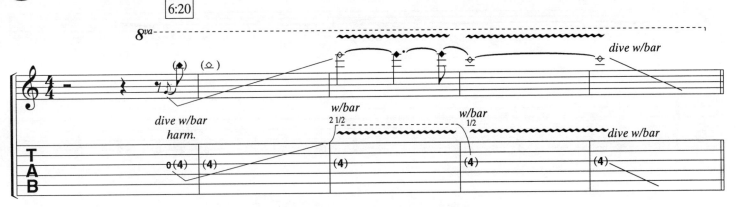

Gradually and smoothly use bar to "pull" harmonic up to pitch indicated.

Wow! Was that an intense whammy-bar work-out or what?! What a great lesson from Dime. His willingness to give away his tricks is praiseworthy since many axemen would definitely choose to keep such a unique trademark a secret if they possibly could. Dime continues to "reveal all" as he answers a batch of questions concerning his noise-making tricks. Read on.

Whammy Pedal Abuse ("Becoming")

Hey Dimebag,
How in the hell do you make that high-pitched sound in "Becoming"? I've heard you use some sort of pedal but I wanna know exactly what you do, from the mouth of the expert. Also, are you using natural harmonics as well as a pedal?
Kim Seabourne
Worcester, England

"I use my DigiTech Whammy pedal set on two octaves up to get that sound. What I do is push the pedal down real quickly on the second beat of each bar of the riff. I'm not hitting any harmonics when I make the squeal happen either; all I'm playing are the octave C notes at the 3rd fret on the A string and the 5th fret of the G string. The whole riff is shown in **Example 112**. When you try it, just move the pedal exactly the way the rig sounds. You may think, 'Oh, man, that's all he's doing?' but just remember, simple can be lethal. So let's get your tone up there crushing and let's have 'Becoming' down there screeching! Come on, let's have it out."

Example 112: "Becoming" main riff

Guitar tuned down one step (low to high: D G C F A D)

All notes sound one step lower than written

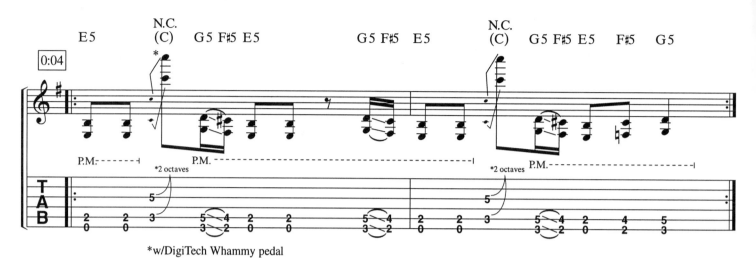

*w/DigiTech Whammy pedal

Hey Dime,

Your column is king, man! My favorite Pantera riff ever is the one in "Becoming" you do with the Whammy pedal. You've shown us how you play it, but my question is How the *#$@ did you come up with it in the first place?

Ken Gilmer
Nashville, TN

"We were jamming around one day on the riff that became 'Becoming' and Phil [Anselmo, vocals] went, 'Make some ****in' noise there, dude,' so I pulled that screech out of my Whammy pedal. It sounded fresh, noisy but controlled, and everybody went, "**** yeah! Why not?!' Also, Vinnie's drum part crushed me when I first heard him play it, and that definitely inspired that riff to happen. I call him the 'electric tap-dancer' because of fast double-bass-drum shit like that."

Dime, my man, I thought you used a pedal to get that high squeal during the main riff in "Becoming," but when I saw you play the song live you weren't stepping on anything. What's the trick, bro?!

Ken "Z Man" Zemanek
Chicago, IL

"The trick is to have a bad-assed guitar tech like Grady [Champion] and let him work his Whammy pedal back there for you so you can dance and jam to the groove instead of being strapped to a pedal! That riff smokes, man, and there's no way I could just stand still on stage in one place while I play it. Grady, if you're reading this, you ****in' rule 88, bud! (Jimmy Johnson! Plus DDS pushing 12 with your name on it! Right back at ya.)"

Chirping Noises

Hey, dude, how did you make the cool-sounding chirping noise that ends your "Hard Line, Sunken Cheeks" [Far Beyond Driven] solo?

Fred Gillis
Seattle, WA

"What I'm doing there is bending the D note at the 15th fret on the high-E string and then tapping the string at the 22nd fret with the edge of my pick while gradually releasing the bend. I start off making a straight up-and-down motion with my pick that gets smaller and smaller as the chop gets faster and faster. Then, once I'm chopping as quick as I can, I start going back and forth with my pick—kinda like I'm sawing the string. If your pick is beat-up a little bit and has some small grooves in it, that'll help out too. To make the trill jump out a hair more on the album, I overdubbed a harmony part to it on another track too."

The Fake Echo in "Walk"
"A bunch of you have written in asking about the fake echo technique I use about two-thirds of the way [3:21–3:23] through my 'Walk' solo. It's real simple, actually; all I'm doing is repeatedly sliding up the G string from the second fret to the 14th fret, using both hands alternately (**Example 113**)."

Example 113: The fake echo lick in "Walk"
Guitar tuned down one step (low to high: D G C F A D)
All notes sound one step lower than written

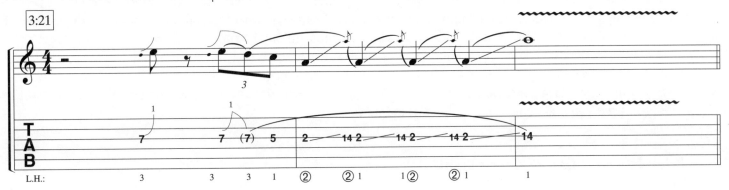

② = middle finger of picking (right) hand

"Here's how it goes, broken down into steps:

➤ **Step 1:** While you're executing the bend at the beginning of the lick, reach over with your right hand (RH) and capo [i.e., fret] the G string at the 2nd fret with your middle finger (**Photo 6**) before you pull-off with the left hand (LH).

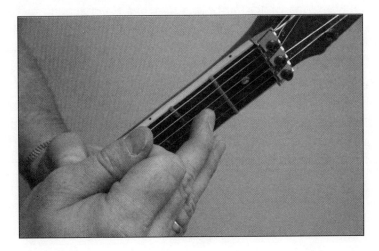

Photo 6: "capoing" the G string
at the 2nd fret with your RH

➤ **Step 2:** As soon as you pull-off with your LH, start sliding your RH-finger up the G string toward the bridge.

➤ **Step 3:** While your RH is sliding, fret the G string at the 2nd fret with your LH.

➤ **Step 4:** When your RH-slide reaches the 14th fret, pull-off and immediately start sliding your LH up the neck.

➤ **Step 5:** While your LH is sliding, fret the G string at the 2nd fret with your RH.

➤ **Step 6:** Pull-off with your LH when it reaches the 14th fret and start sliding your RH up the string, etc.

"Get it? If you don't, check out the 'Walk' video [Vulgar Video] 'cos there's a close-up of me doing this during the solo. If you want to stretch this technique to a new level, try sliding a different note every time instead of repeating the same one. Remember, there are no rules, so dick with shit, experiment and let's get it out here."

Cow-Noise From Hell

Dear Dime,
My band does a cover of "Cowboys From Hell," and thanks to your column I'm nailing the guitar parts pretty good. Trouble is, no matter how hard I try, I can't get that weird noise you make at the very start of the song (just before the main riff comes in) happening. Please tell me how you did that before I lose what's left of my mind!
Joe Bredau
Northport Harbor, NY

"Sometimes it's funny how the first time you play a lick or riff it hits you just right and then it never sounds or feels the same again—that was the case with the 'Cowboys' intro you're talking about. All that weird sound consists of is me just chugging in time on the low-E string running through a cheap echo with the repeat control set on infinite. The trick was getting the effect to catch just right, and I did it no problem on the four-track demo I had put together. Then, when we went in the studio to cut it, I used the same exact echo unit and the same exact everything, but after hours of trying, I couldn't even get it close to the original demo! So, the cool-sounding one I did on my four-track is now the one you hear on the record! That's kind of a little bit of a lesson right there: Always turn a damned recorder on 'cos the first time you nail something could be the only time!"

Good Friends and a Can of Coors Light!

Dear Dime,
I love the way you play and make weird-assed noises on your axe that actually become an integral part of the song as opposed to just being a noise. My all-time favorite batch of noises happens in "Good Friends and a Bottle of Pills" [Far Beyond Driven]—man, they're as sick as Phil's lyrics! How did you make 'em, goddamnit?!
"Psycho B" Rodriguez
Ridge, NY

"Well, Psycho, this almost goes back to the story about the noises at the front of 'Cowboys From Hell.' What was going on with 'Good Friends and a Bottle of Pills' was this: When we were cutting the demo, I was standing right by Vinnie's drums and my [noise] gate was just set tight enough to keep me shut-up. But I had the volume of my guitar turned up full so whenever he hit his snare it would open the gate because my pickups are pretty sensitive. So, every time he hit his snare, it would pop the gate open and let all the racket and shit through my amp.

"Then, when we came to cut it for the album, I stood in the same exact place and it wouldn't do it again no matter what—it just didn't sound as cool! So, we went back and took those noises off the demo! It was real loose on the demo, and some of those noises are me just dicking around, scraping a Coors Light beer can across the strings and just jacking off. Maybe that's what I was missing the second time when we went back to cut it—I didn't have the same amount of beer in my can!"

Chapter II

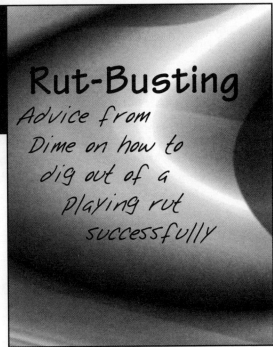

Rut-Busting
Advice from Dime on how to dig out of a playing rut successfully

" Whenever I get down on my playing, I just bend a note, shake it and listen! What I hear sounds so great it makes me realize that even a rut doesn't suck."

Dimebag Darrell

This is one of my all-time favorite *Riffer Madness* columns due to its truly inspirational message. Here our teacher tackles one of the most frustrating things known to six-stringers, getting caught in a rut. More important, he offers some of his patented no-nonsense advice on how to dig yourself out. Take it away, Dime.

Digging Yourself Out of a Playing Rut

"Whenever you find yourself in a rut, always try to remember these two things:

1. You ain't the only dude who gets hit with this shit—we all go through it from time to time.
2. You're not always gonna be stuck there, so don't totally schiz out! The only way that'll happen is if you let it. So don't get bummed out and go '**** it, I quit'—that's a dumb-assed loser attitude. Instead, get to work, man. If you wanna get out of a rut bad enough, it'll happen. It's up to you though—no one else is ever gonna do it for you."

A Simple Solution

"Whenever you find yourself doing the same thing over and over, logic says that the best way out is first, to take a real close look at what you're playing. Then, find out what you keep repeating and say, 'Okay, I won't do that anymore.' At that point, *stop doing it* and try something else instead! I'm not saying you should give up on all your old licks. Just let them rest, and make it your goal to try new things and grow. If you make a definite effort to do this, it'll lead to new ideas and a way out of that rut. Here are some other things that might help you out."

Fatherly Advice

"My dad's a great guitarist, and he said something to me when I was learning to play that I've always remembered. One day I was stomping around the house, all pissed-off because my playing was in a rut. And he said, 'Well, son, if you decided to just learn one new lick a day, how many would you have by the end of the year?' Think about it, man; the possibilities right there are staggering! Shit, if I only knew a lick for *each beer* I've had—I can't imagine how much extra knowledge I'd have!"

The Importance of Others

"To me, a sure-fire way to get *in* a rut is by sitting around playing by yourself for too long. You've gotta get out there and jam, man! You don't necessarily have to be in a band—all you've gotta have are a couple of buds who play too. They don't have to be guitarists either; jamming with a bassist or a drummer is cool. I was real lucky to grow up with a brother that kicks ass on drums. We used to play together all the time, and doing that helped me develop as a guitarist in a BIG way.

"Jamming with other people will create energy and excitement that you can feed off of and that will push you to do things you'd never dream of doing by yourself. I love jamming with my band because the guys inspire me every time. We all get off on each others' playing. Also, whenever I do something that one of 'em likes, he'll say something like, 'Hey, dude, that one note was bad-assed!' Hearing that sort of thing definitely boosts your self-confidence, man! If you play something great in your bedroom, no one's ever gonna say shit about it because no one else heard it!"

Be Yourself, By Yourself

"If you have no buds to jam with, you can always record a rhythm part yourself and then wail lead over it. I used to do that all the time. You don't need to do a whole production deal with a four-track and a drum machine either; all you need is a boom box with a built-in condenser mike and you're set. Don't always solo over the same sort of stuff though, or you could fall into a rut. Whenever I would get tired of soloing over heavy riffs in E, I'd come up with a rhythm part that was in a completely different key and had a completely different feel to it. Then I'd record it and let it take my lead work to a new place. Sometimes a change of mood and pace can help you find fresh ideas, and this is one way of doing that. The laid-back, bluesy B-minor rhythm shown in **Example 114** is a good example of what I'm talking about here."

Example 114: Rut-busting rhythm idea in B minor

Track 99

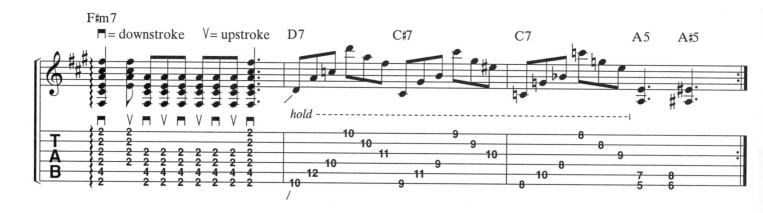

This Sucks? Not!

"Finally, even when you find yourself trapped in the deepest rut you've ever known, don't ever forget just how ****in' good the guitar sounds. Sometimes, because you've been playing so much, it's real easy to take the thing for granted. Never let this happen, Dad! The next time you think, 'Oh, shit, this sucks,' slow down a little bit, take a step back and then take a closer look at things. Whenever I get down on my playing, I just bend a note, shake it and listen! What I hear sounds so great it makes me realize that even a rut doesn't suck. The guitar is a killer-sounding instrument. That's why we play it!

"The next time you're in a rut, just think of me. You'll be out in no time. Bust your sack, C-Cut!"

Chapter 12

Dear Dime

Dime answers a few FAQs (frequently asked questions) from his infamous Feedback Sack!

When Dime offered to answer any questions the readers of Riffer Madness might have, no one was prepared for the avalanche of mail that would ensue. To say the flood-gates opened would be an understatement of epic proportions! Letters literally poured into *Guitar World's* NY HQ by the sackful.

We've already scoped out quite a few of Dime's insightful answers to readers' letters in preceding chapters; below are four more I felt it would be criminal not to include, plus a new one of my very own.

Making a Band Work, On and Off Stage

Dear Dime,
I think it would be way cool if you talked about how Pantera makes it work as a band, both on and off stage. I reckon it would help other bands stay together if they know how you guys do it.

Jim Bernard
Miami, FL

"Man! That's a hard ****in' question to answer 'cos there are a whole bunch of factors you've gotta take into consideration. Basically, a band is just like a family. You gotta make space for each other and understand and respect what the other guys are into 'cos we're not all exactly the same, y'know. Probably the most important thing of all, though, is this: You've all gotta have an honest love for what you're doing if you even want it to halfway happen. Also, if each member of the band doesn't share the same vision to start with, then you'll probably have problems down the road because your goals are gonna be different.

"The way it works with us is that each person kinda plays a different role within the band. It wasn't planned out though; nobody said, 'Okay, I'm gonna be the business man; you be the mediator; you be the whatever.' No one put us in those spots; that's just the way it worked out with us. We always try to help each other rather than go against each other. I guess you could say that being in a band is kinda like a marriage except you've got more than one wife!"

Making It in the Music Biz

Hey Dimebag,
If you've got any tips on getting a record deal or anything else to do with making it in the business, I'd be grateful.
An inspired guitarist,
Jack Fliegler
Phoenix, AZ

"Two words, man—*time* and *endurance*. That's what it takes to get anywhere in this business. We were jamming together for eight or nine years before we got signed, so hang tough and give your shit to as many people as you can. The main thing is to have your own style, and that kinda thing doesn't happen overnight. Hell, it took us nearly eight years to find ourselves and get our 'Cowboys From Hell' identity together. It is possible to get a deal though, I swear—I'm the living proof!"

Playing Live

"As for getting relaxed before going on stage, right off the bat I can tell you this: You don't wanna end up like me, bro! Before I go out and jam, I drink six or so beers and do ten shots of Seagram's 7, but I don't pop any pills or smoke any weed—only kidding! What I really do is this: Once I've done my playing warm-up [see **Chapter 9**] I also like to make sure my whole body is loose. I don't really do any incredible work-out shit; all I do is stretch my body out and get my blood flowing. Then, I just go out there and attack, man! I know a lot of people schiz out when they have to play in front of an audience, and to me that's a waste of energy. What I do is channel all that nervous energy into my jam. If you're playing aggressive stuff like we do, it's pretty easy to do that. So, don't go out there and just pitter about—stomp some ass, m#$%*!#$&*er!"

The Four-Track King

Does this subhead sound familiar? If it does, you've got a good memory 'cos it cropped up way back in **Chapter 2**. The topic at hand is an important one though and, therefore, worth revisiting. As the saying goes, "Repetition is the mother of skill"!

"I can't recommend getting a four-track enough, man. I've used mine every damned day since I got it. It's a total release, and the funny thing is, when you're dicking around with no real pressure, that's when you invariably hit gold. When a riff is written like that, it's definitely in its purest form 'cos it just came out naturally—you weren't sitting around waiting to be creative. That's why I keep going back and extracting riffs from my old four-track tapes. I mean, 'Shedding Skin' [*Far Beyond Driven*] is a four-track from like 40 years ago.

"I've always said that the best way to get better as a player is to jam all you can, whenever you can. But if there ain't other people around to jam with, then a four-track is a great thing to have because you can use it to jam with yourself. Goddamn, you can get one nowadays for like $150. And if you can't afford 150 bucks—which I sure as hell couldn't when I was a kid—do what I used to do and buy or borrow two of those cheap-assed plastic mini-cassette recorders with built-in mikes. Then, record a part on one and jam along with the playback while the other one is recording both parts. Doing this eliminates having to do a mix! And the pay-off is that you get to find and hear parts that mesh together.

"I've pretty much always got a four-track or a pocket recorder with me 'cos you never know when a riff idea is gonna come your way. So, I always try to be prepared to capture them. I've learned the hard way that when you get a killer idea and you go, 'I'll remember that,' and start messing with it later on, it just ain't the same. You gotta get it on tape right away."

Seven Strings? Use 'Em or Lose One!

Hey Dime,
What's your take on the seven-string guitar craze that's been so dominant in many of the heavy bands that rose to prominence in the late '90s?

Nick Bowcott
Stony Brook, NY

"Hey, man, I don't mean to be a preacher, but I gotta tell it like it is. If you've got a seven-string guitar and you use only the bottom two or three strings, why the hell have a seven-string when you ain't even using six? Why not just use a three- or four-string guitar like Scott Ian does? Most dudes who use seven-string sound no different to someone who's playing a six-string tuned down.

"For me to fully express myself on guitar, I can't just go chunking around on the bottom strings all the time. Don't get me wrong, there's power in that and I can see how someone can get off on that. Hell, I do it too! But if that's all you do, it becomes a real one-dimensional kinda thing. If you wanna make the guitar really sing and talk for you, then you can't be scared of those little strings, man; they're there to be used so you've gotta step up to 'em! Grab a hold of one of those high notes and bend that mother****er all over the neck. Let it feedback, pull on that whammy bar and use every goddamned thing you've got at your disposal.

"I realize that the day of the guitar hero isn't shining anything as bright as it was in the '80s, but lead guitar ain't gone away like everyone says it has. I may not do as many solos as I used to, but I still do 'em when the song calls for it. I've got nothing against any of the new bands, but some of them don't play any solos—period. Face it, man, you've gotta have some lead-playing going on—it's a vital part of kick-ass, full-meal-deal, heavy music. Rhythm may be the teeth of the machine, but leads are the personality and heart of the individual. You can reach different parts of the soul with it."

Epilogue
Uplift and C-Cut!
Unlucky for us, the end of the book!
A parting inspirational shot from Dime as he says, "Lata!"

Well, friends, fans and family! It's come time for me to say 'C-cut'—for a while. I sincerely hope you've enjoyed and picked up on all the stuff we've covered. Damn, we've gone through a buttload of cool techniques, knowledge and straight-out crazy shit, including some trick stuff I'm sure most blacksmiths would never reveal or uncover! I'm glad I could and would do this for the simple reason that there's more where all that came from. I hope I've helped open some ears and eyes! Let all the ideas I've put in your head come as they will—subconsciously and naturally. And, remember, it's all good, everything goes and there ain't no damned rules or boundaries. So get off! Tear it a fresh ass, tear it hard, rip gaping holes in it! Make tracks, leave marks!

"Forever stronger than all."

Dimebag Darrell

Appendix I
Discography

As mentioned in **Chapter 2,** all four albums in this section were released on the band's own label, **Metal Magic Records and Tapes** (MMR). Interestingly enough, prior to recording the fourth one, *Power Metal*, the band signed a deal with Gold Mountain Records, a label distributed by the mighty Atlantic Records. When Atlantic heard the album, however, they felt it was too heavy, and so Gold Mountain gave Pantera the rights to release *Power Metal* and eventually let the band go altogether—more fool them! What makes this story even more amusing/ironic is the fact that Atco, the label that signed a much heavier Dime & Co. a mere two years later, was also a subsidiary of Atlantic!

Metal Magic
(MMR, 1983)
Darrell Abbott (guitar)
Vinnie Paul Abbott (drums)
Rex Rocker (bass)
Terry Glaze (vocals)

Track Listing
1. Ride My Rocket
2. I'll Be Alright
3. Tell Me if You Want It
4. Latest Lover
5. Biggest Part of Me
6. Metal Magic
7. Widowmaker
8. Nothin' On (But the Radio)
9. Sad Lover
10. Rock Out

Projects in the Jungle
(MMR, 1984)

Track Listing
1. All Over Tonight
2. Out for Blood
3. Blue Lite Turnin' Red
4. Like Fire
5. In Over My Head
6. Projects in the Jungle
7. Heavy Metal Rules!
8. Heartbeat Away
9. Killers
10. Takin' My Life

I am the Night
(MMR, 1985)

Track Listing
1. Hot and Heavy
2. I Am the Night
3. Onward We Rock
4. D.G.T.T.M.
5. Daughters of the Queen
6. Down Below
7. Come-on Eyes
8. Right on the Edge
9. Valhalla
10. Forever Tonight

Power Metal
(1988)
Darrell Lance (guitar)
Vinnie Paul (drums)
Rex Rocker (bass)
Philip Anselmo (vocals)

Track Listing
1. Rock the World
2. Power Metal
3. We'll Meet Again
4. Over and Out
5. Proud to Be Loud*
6. Down Below
7. Death Trap
8. Hard Ride
9. Burnnn!
10. P*S*T*88

*Written by Mark Ferrari

Section II: The major leagues!
(*Cowboys From Hell* to present) 1990–2000

Cowboys From Hell
(Atco Records, 1990)
Produced & Engineered by Terry Date
Co-Produced by Pantera

Track Listing
1. Cowboys From Hell (4:06)
2. Primal Concrete Sledge (2:13)
3. Psycho Holiday (5:19)
4. Heresy (4:45)
5. Cemetary Gates (7:03)
6. Domination (5:02)
7. Shattered (3:21)
8. Clash With Reality (5:15)
9. Medicine Man (5:15)
10. Message in Blood (5:09)
11. The Sleep (5:47)
12. The Art of Shredding (4:16)

All songs written & arranged by Pantera

Vulgar Display of Power
(Atco Records, 1992)
Produced & Engineered & Mixed by Terry Date & Vinnie Paul
Co-Produced by Pantera

Track Listing
1. Mouth for War (3:56)
2. A New Level (2:57)
3. Walk (5:15)
4. Fucking Hostile (2:49)
5. This Love (6:32)
6. Rise (4:36)
7. No Good (Attack the Radical) (4:50)
8. Live in a Hole (4:59)
9. Regular People (Conceit) (5:27)
10. By Demons Be Driven (4:39)
11. Hollow (5:45)

All songs written & arranged by Pantera

Far Beyond Driven
(Eastwest Records America, 1994)
Produced & Engineered & Mixed by Terry Date & Vinnie Paul
Co-Produced by Pantera

Track Listing
1. Strength Beyond Strength (3:39)
2. Becoming (3:05)
3. 5 Minutes Alone (5:50)
4. I'm Broken (4:25)
5. Good Friends and a Bottle of Pills (2:54)
6. Hard Lines, Sunken Cheeks (7:01)
7. Slaughtered (3:57)
8. 25 Years (6:06)
9. Shedding Skin (5:37)
10. Use My Right Arm (4:52)
11. Throes of Rejection (5:01)
12. Planet Caravan* (4:04)

All songs written & arranged by Pantera except * written by Frank Iommi, John Osbourne, William Ward & Terence Butler (a.k.a. Black Sabbath!)

The Great Southern Trendkill
(Eastwest Records America, 1996)
Produced & Engineered & Mixed by Terry Date & Vinnie Paul
Co-Produced by Pantera
Also Recorded by Ulrich Wild

Track Listing
1. The Great Southern Trendkill (3:46)
2. War Nerve (4:53)
3. Drag the Waters (4:55)
4. 10'S (4:49)
5. 13 Steps to Nowhere (3:37)
6. Suicide Note Pt. I (4:44)
7. Suicide Note Pt. II (4:19)
8. Living Through Me (Hell's Wrath) (4:50)
9. Floods (6:59)
10. The Underground in America (4:33)
11. (Reprise) Sandblasted Skin (3:24/5:39)*

*The track fades out at 3:24 and then, after 1:36 of silence, starts slowly fading back in at 5:00 before finally finishing at 5:39

All songs written & arranged by Pantera

Official Live: 101 Proof

(Eastwest Records America, 1997)
Produced by Vinnie Paul &
Dimebag Darrell

Track Listing
1. New Level (4:24)
2. Walk (5:50)
3. Becoming (3:59)
4. 5 Minutes Alone (5:36)
5. Sandblasted Skin (4:29)
6. Suicide Note Pt.2 (4:20)
7. War Nerve (5:21)
8. Strength Beyond Strength (3:37)
9. Domination/Hollow (3:43)
10. This Love (6:57)
11. I'm Broken (4:27)
12. Cowboys From Hell (4:35)
13. Cemetary Gates (7:53)
14. Hostile (3:56)
15. Where You Come From* (5:11)
16. I Can't Hide* (2:16)

*Studio recording May '97, previously
unreleased

All songs written & arranged by
Pantera

_____

Reinventing the Steel

(Eastwest Records America, 2000)
Produced by Vinnie Paul &
Dimebag Darrell
Co-Produced by Sterling Winfield

Track Listing
1. Hellbound (2:40)
2. Goddamn Electric (4:56)
3. Yesterday Don't Mean Shit (4:19)
4. You've Gotta Belong to It (4:13)
5. Revolution Is My Name (5:15)
6. Death Rattle (3:17)
7. We'll Grind That Axe for a Long
   Time (3:44)
8. Uplift (3:45)
9. It Makes Them Disappear (6:21)
10. I'll Cast a Shadow (5:22)

All songs written & arranged by
Pantera

_____

Other recordings by Pantera or Dimebag that are out there, not hard to get and worth checking out:

Note: This listing doesn't include hard-to-get (and no doubt expensive!) or redundant (tracks already on Pantera albums anyway) stuff like:

- For radio-only edits (e.g., the "Suicide Note, Pt.1 [Live Through This Night Remix Edit]").
- Versions of already released songs that have since appeared on soundtrack albums (e.g., the edited version of "Cemetary Gates" that appeared on the *Demon Night Soundtrack* and "Where You Come From" on the *Strange Land Soundtrack*).
- Any rare B-sides/remixes/live stuff that may have been released outside of America (e.g., the Japanese *Walk EP* that featured remixes of "Walk" [2], "Fucking Hostile" and "By Demons Be Driven" plus live versions of "Cowboys From Hell" and "Heresy").
- Any "Tribute to Pantera" albums (so far I've seen two and both featured a slew of bands I've never heard of!).
- Stuff you'd never be able to get your hands on for neither love nor money (unless you're incredibly lucky or well connected). For example, Dime's guest appearance (as "Diamond Darrell") on the hysterical Darrell-penned track, "C&W Transvestite," which appeared on a 1992 demo tape by the band Throbbin' Rodd (a four-piece featuring W.Axl Rodd on bass and Fishin' Rodd on drums!).

That said, here's the listing in no particular order:

"Immortally Insane" [*Heavy Metal 2000 Soundtrack*] by Pantera
A previously unreleased Pantera cut that (surprise, surprise) kicks major ass!

"The Badge" [*The Crow Soundtrack*] by Pantera
"It's a song by an Oregon-based band called Poison Idea," Dime reveals. "It was Phil's idea to do this tune 'cos he was always cranking it backstage before shows. It was the first cover we ever recorded, and I like how it turned out because it doesn't sound like any of our records—it's got a lot of cut on the top, it's got teeth all over it."
Note: This track also appeared as a B-side on a vinyl (yes, vinyl!) 7" single of "5 Minutes Alone." Is this hard to get? You betcha!

"Cat Scratch Fever" [*Detroit Rock City Soundtrack*] by Pantera
A blistering cover of Ted Nugent's classic cut by Dime & Co.

"Electric Funeral" [*Nativity in Black II: A Tribute to Black Sabbath*] by Pantera
A far beyond excellent cover and the definite high point of this album. No wonder *Hit Parade* magazine recently referred to Pantera as "the best heavy metal band on the planet"!

"Heard It on the X" [*ECW Extreme Music*] by Tres Diablos
Who are Tres Diablos? Dime, Vinnie and Rex, that's who! Their version of this ZZ Top staple is one of the highlights of this album. "Me and Rex actually traded off vocals, just like Billy and Dusty do in ZZ," Dime tells us. "'Heard It on the X' is just one of those tunes that always comes on when you're sitting around drunk, and makes you think, 'Damn, that'd be a kick-ass song to redo sometime.' So, we did!"
Interesting Note: Also featured on this album is a cover of Pantera's "Walk" by Kilgore

"Fractured Mirror" [*Spacewalk: A Salute to Ace Frehley*] by Dimebag Darrell
"The people doin' the record faxed me a couple of times about this, but I was moving at the time so they didn't hear from me," Dime recalls. "Then my manager called me up and told me that Ace himself really wanted me to do it, so I just said, 'Yes, sir!'"

"King Size" and "Riding Shotgun" [*Stomp 442*] by Anthrax, lead guitar by Dimebag
Dime's pals in Anthrax asked him if he'd like to play lead on a couple of tracks, and he happily obliged. "I flew to New York in the afternoon, kicked some balls, got drunk with 'em and then flew back home on the red-eye," he recalls. Scott Ian & Co. were so delighted with Dime's contribution that they gave him a big-screen TV as a thank-you. Not bad pay for a few hours' work!

"Born Again Idiot" and "Inside Out" [*The Threat Is Real*] by Anthrax, lead guitar by Dimebag
Once again, Darrell steps in and lends Anthrax a lead-playing hand in his own inimitable fashion. I guess he now owns two big-screen TVs!

"Caged in a Rage" [*Supercop Soundtrack*] by Dimebag Darrell
This is the first and, at the time of writing (August 2000), only Dimebag "solo" release. Will there be more? "There's more to my guitar-playing than what I do in Pantera," Dime reveals. "I jam and dick around on my four-track all the time, man. Man, I've got thousands of songs I've done on my four-track—some are humorous and some are serious. If my liver don't give out on me, then maybe I'll get around to putting some of my four-track stuff out there to show some of the other sides of my play."

Also hard to get but well worth a listen:

"Believer" [*Randy Rhoads Tribute*] featuring Dimebag on lead guitar
This tribute album to the late, great Randy Rhoads was released in Japan in 2000 and also features solos by the likes of George Lynch, Jake E. Lee and ex-Accept man Wolf Hoffmann. To be frank though, most of the lead breaks are extremely disappointing because they stray too far away from Randy's original brilliance. As the saying goes, "If it ain't broke, don't fix it!" Dime's "Believer" solo, however, is the shining exception to this sad rule. Darrell plays a blazing version of the solo and pretty much nails it note-for-note—and, in so doing, truly pays tribute to one of his guitar heroes! The vocalist on "Believer"? Dime's old ex-Skid Row pal, Sebastian Bach.

Appendix II
About the Author, Special Thanks, etc.

About the Author

English born and bred, Nick Bowcott was the founder, guitarist and riff-writer of the mid-'80s cult heavy metal band Grim Reaper. He's also a southpaw—but please don't hold that against him! Grim Reaper released three albums on RCA America in the mid-'80s—*See You in Hell* (1984), *Fear No Evil* (1985) and *Rock You to Hell* (1987)—all of which grazed the Top 100 of the Billboard Album Chart.

As you'd expect, with a name like Grim Reaper and a bunch of songs with "hell" in the title, this was a band that most critics loved to hate. Of the many slammings the band received, a review that stated "listening to this record was as pleasurable as giving myself a frontal lobotomy with a blunt butter knife" was a definite high point. Another was being voted one of "The 10 Worst Bands of the '80s" by the now-defunct *Creem* magazine. Nick & Co. were so delighted with the latter that they sent the female author a dozen black roses as a thank-you. Hey, all press is good press—right?! This said, not all the reviews were horrible. In fact, in a recent review of the 1999 *Best of Grim Reaper* CD, in the magazine *Metal Attack*, the following was written: "as far as southpaw six-stringers go, everybody points to [Tony] Iommi [of Black Sabbath], and rightly so, but Bowcott came up with some pretty impressive work in his own right." Bowcott adamantly denies that any money changed hands regarding this review.

As far as Nick is concerned, bad reviews and being compared to Spinal Tap aside, the definite high point of Reaper's run was an appearance in front of 83,000 people at the 1985 Texxas Jam at the Cotton Bowl in Dallas, Texas. "Playing to an audience of that size is something every band dreams of—unless they're complete liars," Bowcott states. "It was an unforgettable experience that was made even more memorable by the fact that we went down well and no one threw anything at us!"

Grim Reaper's career was cut short in 1988 when a totally bogus lawsuit was filed against them by their initial record company Ebony Records—a tin-pot, one-man operation. The case was eventually thrown out of court after five years, but by that time the band's time had come and gone. On a happier note, a major British TV news show exposed the owner of Ebony Records for the rip-off merchant he was. The result? As a direct result of said broadcast, within weeks Ebony was declared bankrupt because no one would do business with them.

By the time Grim Reaper's run came grinding to an unexpected halt, Nick had already established himself as a journalist specializing in "analyzing heavy metal/hard rock guitar-playing." His popular monthly "Guitar Clinic" for *Circus* magazine (which was huge in the '80s) clocked up a staggering 100 articles, and he wrote some 40 articles for the English magazine, *Guitarist*, including nine front-cover features. In 1990 he joined the staff of *Guitar World* magazine, specializing in "private lessons" with guitar heroes—a task he still carries out on a monthly basis with much enjoyment to this very day. "Basically, they have me sit down with the likes of Tony Iommi, Dimebag, Billy Gibbons, Kirk Hammett, Angus Young and Kerry King while they show me exactly how they play their classic riffs and solos—and they pay me for it too!" Nick laughs. "Sometimes life is good."

Nick also writes regularly for the English magazine Guitar; has done a six-hour teaching tape course for Hotlicks entitled *The Heavy Metalist* and a teaching video for Hal Leonard Publishing called *Crash Course in Brutality*; and has also penned a book for the latter company titled *Hell Bent for Lead Licks: A Guitarist's Guide to Judas Priest*.

In addition to all of his journalistic work, Nick has a real job working for Marshall Amplification USA/Korg USA. He started in 1992 as a product specialist, a job that kept him on the road doing guitar clinics all over America. Then, in 1996, he was promoted to the position of U.S. product manager for Marshall—a job he still does with pride to this very day.

Nick is married and has three kids, a dog, a rabbit, two parrots, a bunch of fish and, much to his wife's chagrin, some 20 guitars. Thanks to what he does, he gets to hang out with the likes of Slash, Zakk Wylde and Dimebag on a regular basis and call it work! When asked who her favorite guitarist is, his oldest child, a pretty little five-year-old girl ("She looks like her mum—thank God!" Nick states) named Paige, simply smiles and says, "Darrell." Enough said.

The "I Owe You Big Time" Roll Call of Honor (?!)

Aaron Stang at Warner Bros. Publications for having the patience of Job (hopefully the wait for this was worth it!); Walter O'Brien and Kim Zide at Concrete management for being so damned cool; Grady Champion for technical assistance; Guy Sykes for numerous passes and getting me back to my Tokyo hotel when I was Black-Tooth-Grinned outta my tree; Dime, Vinnie, Rex and Philip for crushing music, countless killer shows, killer hospitality and friendship; Rita for some amazing steaks at Camp Strapped; and Boddingtons, Abbotts, Ruddles, Old Speckled Hen and Dead Guy Ale for inspiration; Rob Roscigno for the excellent hand photos and the killer D1600 tips; and Mike "Grim Reaper sucked and you owe me beers" Venezia of Musicland for the loan of the boss "Whammy pedal" equivalent for the recording of the "Becoming" riff.

Extra special thanks and love go to my wife Tara and my three kids—Paige, Jarod and Aiden. All four of 'em, and especially Tara, somehow put up with me trashing the house for months on end while I wrote and researched this friggin' book. Without you guys, I'd be nothing. You rule, and I love you all to bits.

The ultimate thanks, however, goes to the man with the red goatee himself—Dimebox Danny! Hey, bro, thanx for the crushing riffs, smokin' solos and God knows how many hangovers! Thanx also for your infectious enthusiasm, your warped sense of humor, your unique way of explaining things and, most important, your friendship. Don't ever change, amigo—metal needs you!

This book is respectfully dedicated in loving memory to my father, John T. Bowcott. If it wasn't for the faith and support he and my dear mother (hi Mum!) have given to anything and everything I've followed with a genuine passion (regardless of what they thought), none of the above would've ever happened. Sadly, he passed away before this tome was finished. He probably wouldn't have approved of some of the language, but I'm sure he would've been proud as punch anyway because of the true spirit in which it was written. I hope you like the book, Dad. Thanx for everything, and rest in peace. Your memory lives fondly on in my heart and always will.

Photo of book author and co-author/subject taken in early 1996 at Dime's Camp Strapped studio just after The Great Southern Trendkill... album was recorded. Note the highly unusual use of a Marshall Micro-Stack!

"He is the best of the new generation and, most important, like the rest of Pantera, he really believes in what he's doing."

Tony Iommi, Black Sabbath

"I just want to say Darrell is a hell of a drinker and a hell of a player!"

Kirk Hammett, Metallica

"Dimebag's probably the best in the game. He's one of the few guys putting out music that interests me anymore because he hasn't forgotten what angry, chunky riffs are. He's a cool dude, great in all aspects of playing his axe and very fond of his booze. Other than that, he sucks! (Just kidding, bro!)"

Kerry King, Slayer

"Dimebag Darrell—what else can you say? That name brings up nothing but thoughts of a true player (technically and creatively), performer, entertainer and a straight-up party animal! Changed my path as a player the minute I first heard Pantera."

Stephen Carpenter, Deftones

"In my generation of guitar players, he's the best one I've seen or heard in the last 15 years. He really does have it all. He's not just a lead player and he's not just a rhythm player—first and foremost, he's a songwriter who writes great stuff. All of his amazing technical ability is secondary to that."

Scott Ian, Anthrax & SOD

"He's one hell of a cool dude and a mother$%*#er on guitar. He comes up with some monster riffs with a touch of good-ol'-boy flavor. Even though he's very talented on the solo side of playing, he doesn't feel the need to overload every lead with technical shit. You can hear on some solos that he's just having fun, making *#$%in' noise. Besides all that, you have to respect a guy who can drink like me and Kerry!"

Jeff Hanneman, Slayer

"Dimebag? Aside from being able to drink his ass off, he can play the living crap out his fiddle as well. I'm proud to call him a ~~friend~~ drinking partner. The next beer is on me, brother!"

Zakk Wylde, Black Label Society

"He's a whisky-drinkin', harmonic-squealin' Texas red-beard who's 'ringing like hell'!"
Mike Tempesta (a.k.a. M33), Powerman 5000

"Pantera and Dimebag in particular really changed the whole way I viewed metal and what it could be. His guitar tone really made me totally re-examine what I was doing, and I used to listen to their first record for hours trying to match my guitar tone to it. He was also the first one that made me realize that a noise gate was essential for the sound I was aiming for. If that's not enough, he's a cool guy too!"

Wayne Static, Static-X